Essays Into Literacy

Other books by Frank Smith

The Genesis of Language (edited, with George A. Miller)
Understanding Reading (three editions)
Psycholinguistics and Reading
Comprehension and Learning
Reading Without Nonsense (published under the title *Reading* in the U.K.)
Writing and the Writer
Awakening to Literacy (edited, with Hillel Goelman and Antoinette A. Oberg)

Essays Into Literacy
Selected Papers and Some Afterthoughts

Frank Smith

HEINEMANN
Portsmouth • Oxford

Heinemann
361 Hanover Street
Portsmouth, NH 03801-3912
A Division of Reed Publishing (USA) Inc.
Offices and agents throughout the world

Irwin Publishing, Concord, Ontario
ISBN 0-7725-0020-7

First published 1983

Library of Congress Cataloging in Publication Data

Smith, Frank, 1928-
  Essays into literacy.

  1. Reading—Addresses, essays, lectures.   2. Literacy—
Addresses, essays, lectures.   3. Language arts—
Addresses, essays, lectures.   I. Title.
LB1050.S5728   1983   428.4   83-8454
ISBN   0-435-08205-1
ISBN   0-435-10817-4 (UK)

Cover design by Ryan Cooper

Printed in the United States of America

93 94 95 96 97 98   14 13 12 11 10 9

Contents

Introduction

Literacy is a broad and still largely unexplored terrain with many entrances and exits. Linguists, psychologists, sociologists, anthropologists, educators, administrators, and other specialists have made familiar trails without necessarily crossing each other's path. Individual vantage points—including my own—may offer only limited views.

My essays into literacy have been digressive, helped perhaps, by the fact that I have been led by no specific concern beyond my own questions about language and learning. I have no ambition to develop a commercial reading or writing program; I am reluctant to tell teachers what they should do; and I am too realistic to expect to change the world. I find language fascinating and have felt free to meander through its landscapes, guided by chance and my own instincts, wandering away from beaten tracks, following trails if they appear to promise rewarding perspectives and giving them up when they become dead ends.

The thirteen papers that I have selected for the present volume were written over a period of 10 years, when I also wrote half a dozen books on a similar range of topics. The books are milestones of organized journeys, major enterprises planned in advance. The papers are written more spontaneously; they are more immediate reactions to opportunities, provocations, and developing ideas. The papers do more than fill in the seams between books. They reflect the unplanned and unanticipated changes of emphasis and direction of my thoughts, and so are prospective rather than retrospective.

I shall not attempt to trace a progression of my thought through the papers or the years in which they were written. Progression is not the appropriate word, I think, despite the popular use of linear and sequential terms like *progression*, *process*, and *development* in cognitive and developmental psychology. Rather, I see myself circling around a broad range of topics and interests, closing in to investigate particular questions or issues. I am surprised to find that traces of ideas that I think are my most recent— such as the political rather than theoretical basis of many critical educational problems, and the inappropriateness of many of our common educational metaphors—can be found in articles I wrote years ago and, no doubt, earlier still in other people's writings.

Sometimes I think that agricultural metaphors might be far more appropriate to describe what happens to writers—such as fields lying fallow, crops being rotated, seeds being planted, dormant periods, fertilization, taking root, branching, grafting, transplanting, and harvesting.

In the first two papers in this collection, the emphasis on teachers and their concerns is a response to requests urged on me rather than my own preferences. The focus on reading in the next few papers (Chapters 3 through 5 and 7) is a direct consequence of the kinds of courses I was teaching and the research in which I was involved at the time. It was only after a few years (paradoxically, perhaps, by the time I had become characterized as an expert in "reading") that I felt free to spend more time writing about my wider concerns in language and education. I was able to take a closer look at language generally (Chapters 6 and 8), at writing (Chapter 9), and even at talking to oneself (Chapter 10). During the past 2 or 3 years, I have been able to reconsider the whole matter of learning and education (Chapters 11 and 12) and eventually to question the conceptual basis of my original approaches (Chapter 13).

The papers appear in roughly the sequence in which they were written, which is not always the order in which they appeared in print. They appear as they were published, except for the elimination of repetitions, correction of literals, and other editorial matters. The only exception is Chapter 1, from which I have removed entire sentences because I did not like them.

At the end of this book, under the guise of responding to questions frequently provoked by ideas in these papers, I have taken the opportunity to elaborate on some points that the papers obviously do not cover adequately.

Usually, I resist definitions, which often are either doomed attempts to legislate how language shall be used or unnecessary restrictions on what can be discussed. However, perhaps I should say what I believe *literacy* to mean—that is, the ability to make use of all available possibilities of written language. By *using written language* I mean making sense of it, and using it to make sense of the world, as well as producing it.

I do not see how there can be (nor that there should be) such a thing as *minimal literacy*; this seems a contradiction in terms, like *narrow broadmindedness*. Literacy is like boats and telescopes, useful but not restricted to utilitarian ends. To teach reading and writing as if their most important uses were for completing tax returns and job applications is like using a telescope as a doorstop.

Reading and writing can be used for exploration, experience, and discovery. They create worlds. As I often have argued, both reading and writing generate possibilities and ideas for the individual which might otherwise never exist. This is how I have tried to use written language in the papers that follow.

F.S.
Victoria, B.C.

1
The Politics of Ignorance

In "The Politics of Reading," Postman (1973) suggests that schools should relinquish their concern with written language literacy—which he thinks is "political"—especially since a poor job is made of reading instruction and electronic communications technology has made written language obsolete. While I shall briefly argue that Postman's pronouncements are ill-founded, my major purpose will be to place the issue of literacy within a far more general context.

Postman addresses himself to a *symptom* of the malaise that afflicts our schools, not to the cause. His electronic panacea would aggravate the complaint rather than cure it. I see only one political issue in education—and only one educational issue in politics—an issue that, for want of a better word, can be called *ignorance*. The question is not whether schools should try to inculcate reading—or any other skill—in students, but the extent to which they should contaminate children with the most contagious of social diseases, mental stultification.

Children do not arrive at school ignorant, though they may arrive illiterate. Whether or not they leave school illiterate, they frequently leave it ignorant, which is the state in which the more "successful" of them may enter universities and other institutions of higher ignorance, some in due course to return to the classroom and spread the infection to another generation of children.

The Ignorance Explosion

First, let us consider critical attributes of ignorance. Ignorance is not a matter of not knowing, but of not knowing that you don't know or mistakenly believing that you do know or that at least some expert somewhere does know. Ignorance is not so much not knowing an answer as not knowing that there is a question, not being able to think when thinking is required. Ignorance is a blind dependence that someone else will be able to tell you what to do.

There is far more ignorance in the world today than ever before. Contemporary men and women find themselves in many

Reprinted with permission from Sister Rosemary Winklejohann (Ed.), *The Politics of Reading*. Newark, Delaware: IRA/ERIC, 1973. Neil Postman's article "The Politics of Reading" also appears in Winklejohann's book.

more situations in which they believe they have or expect to be given solutions that in fact are nonexistent or constitute more complex problems. Where once there was uncertainty about how to organize the economy of feudal villages, in today's cities we are totally ignorant about making life bearable or even possible. Once we wrestled with the problem of winning local wars; today we have no idea how to survive peace. Limited transportation was once an unavoidable inconvenience; today the automobile chokes us. In place of occasional famine we eat foods essentially devoid of nourishment. Once we knew no better than to allow sewage to befoul the streets. Today we have invented so many kinds of artificial excrement that neither the oceans nor the air around us can accommodate it. Schools were once unsure about the best use of slate, a modest ignorance which contemporary technology has expanded through an incredible range of electronic gadgetry. The intelligence of the world is boggling under the brunt of what is incautiously called "information" that makes it just about impossible to separate the true from the false, the real from the fantastic, the relevant from the rubbish. Our environment is clogged with nonsense.

But while ignorance abounds, it is by no means uniformly distributed. Ignorance is directly related to what you need to know, or to what you presume to know. The villager may not be able to direct the tourist to the nearest roadhouse, but it is not the villager who is lost. The doctor is ignorant, not the patient, if the diagnosis is in doubt. And as I have already asserted, children do not come to school ignorant. The majority arrive ready, willing, and able to learn. They have already resolved intellectual problems of astounding complexity, should we pause to think about it, ranging from mastering a language to organizing a coherent theory of the world around them, including their own place in it. They are adept at making sense of the world, at relating what is new to what they know already. They can cope.

Long before infants acquire control of their bladders they demonstrate an intellectual awareness, flexibility, and responsiveness that is the very antithesis of ignorance. Children can think long before they come to school. The first time most children meet nonsense in their lives is in the classrooms (some basal reading systems pride themselves on the fact that their content is meaningless). Learning is not meaningful to many children in school, any more than teaching is meaningful to many teachers. The first lesson that many children learn is "Don't think, do as I tell you," just as the teachers themselves have been taught

"Don't think, someone else will tell you what to do" (the concept of "leadership"). But I am getting ahead of my argument. As I was saying, ignorance is not distributed equally in this world. It is relative to the situation you are in, a function of your aspirations and expectations. In particular, ignorance is clustered in our educational institutions.

Ignorance in Education

Two kinds of ignorance may be distinguished in education, which I shall label soft-core and hard-core. Soft-core ignorance, which tends to be found in schools, is the ignorance of those who feel they need to be told what to do. Many teachers are trained to be ignorant, to rely on the opinions of experts or "superiors" rather than on their own judgment. The questions I am asked after lectures to teachers on the topic of reading are always eminently *practical*—how should reading be taught, which method is best, and what should be done about a real-life child of 8 who has the devastating misfortune to read like a statistically fictitious child of 6? Teachers do not ask the right kind of question. Instead of inquiring what they should *do*, which can never be answered with the generality they expect, they should ask what they need to *know* in order to decide for themselves. (It is a monument to the efficiency of the brainwashing that teachers receive during their training that they are practically immune to insult on the topic of their own intellectual capacity. They only express surprise or disbelief when it is suggested that their own experience and intuition might be as good a guide for action as the dogma of some expert.)

Soft-core ignorance is not restricted to teachers. It is reflected at all levels of education in the pathetic faith that electronic technology will provide the answers to all problems (instead of creating more problems). A senior officer of the International Reading Association recently waxed lyrical regarding his board's joint exploration with the Boeing Aerospace Group of "the possible applications of space-age telecommunications technology to help eradicate world illiteracy"—as if space engineers must be privy to some cabalistic knowledge about teaching reading. Man may not have got to the moon before the age of computers and systems analysis, but children have been learning to read for centuries. Every method of teaching reading ever devised has worked with some children (which only goes to prove how adaptable children are). We do not need to find something different to do in the future, but rather to discover what we have been doing right in the past. We talk as if it were a miracle that any child ever learns to read. But if we think about the facility with which most "illiterates" learned to talk, it might appear more remarkable that educators are able to arrange an environment in which so many children consistently fail to learn to read.

Soft-core ignorance, then, is the expectation that someone else can be relied upon to solve your practical problems and save you the trouble of thinking. Hard-core ignorance, on the other hand, is the belief that you know the answers to all problems and can do the thinking for other people. And hard-core ignorance is concentrated at the upper levels of our educational hierarchy (I use the term in its literal sense of a priesthood), notably in the universities.

In my experience, the promiscuity with which teachers are willing to be seduced by some overqualified outsider is exceeded only by the avidity with which academics from a range of totally irrelevant disciplines have their intellectual way with teachers. Nowhere is ignorance of the reading process more pronounced than among the linguists, psychologists, systems analysts, and brain surgeons who are prepared to tell reading teachers how to teach reading.

Some Specifics of Educational Ignorance

After such generalities, I shall now talk briefly about ignorance with respect to reading, reading instruction, electronic instructional technology, and the role of schools, all of which will give an opportunity to make at least a few points relevant to the Postman article.

Reading is an obscure topic enveloped in a dense fog of pedagogical mystique and mythology. Learning to read is frequently confused with reading instruction; the vast majority of books on "reading" or the psychology thereof are thinly disguised tracts of instructional dogma. It is a typical teacher's error to confuse what is done in school with what a child learns. The most that can be said for any method of reading instruction that succeeds—and, as I have said, all methods succeed with some children—is that somebody must be doing something right. More dangerous are the widespread beliefs that a child will not learn unless told exactly what to do (which is obviously and fortunately false, because no one knows enough about reading to tell a child what to do) and that there must be something wrong with a child who does not learn to read.

There is a good deal to say about reading that I have no space to elaborate upon here. I shall list just a few points to give a flavor of them, and perhaps to whet an appetite or two. Reading is not primarily decoding to sound, nor do the eyes play a primary role in reading. Reading by "phonics" is demonstrably impossible (ask any computer). Reading places an impossible burden upon the visual system and upon memory unless the reader is able to read fast, without an undue concern for literal accuracy and with comprehension as immediate as it is for spoken language. Memorization interferes with comprehension, and so do "comprehension tests." Children learn to read by reading, and the sensible teacher makes reading easy and interesting, not difficult and boring.

I shall make four blanket assertions that I regard as easily defensible; the fact that they are widely ignored and even suppressed in education would be a prime argument for the prosecution if I were trying to convict schools of criminal ignorance: A child does not need to be very intelligent to learn to read. A child does not need to be very mature to learn to read. A child does not need to come from a socially or economically superior home, or to have literate parents, in order to learn to read. A child does not need to wait to get to school to learn to read.

Most teachers of reading *know* the preceding statements are true, even if they are not familiar with published sources like Durkin, Fowler, Moore, and Torrey. But in any case, if you think intelligence, maturity, "experience," and skilled adult supervision are necessary for learning to read, how do you think an infant learns the much more complex skills of spoken language? As many parents in North America are discovering, children have a reading problem only if they are still unable to read when they get to school.

In short, all the evidence indicates that it is not so much inadequacy on the part of children that makes learning to read such a hassle as the way in which we expect them to learn—through instructional procedures that systematically deprive them of relevant practice and necessary information. The more difficulty children experience in learning to read, the less reading and the more nonsense drills we typically arrange for them to do.

Rather than pausing to reflect upon where the fault really lies, however, it is becoming fashionable these days to respond with a "what-the-hell, what's the need for children to learn to read in any case" attitude. Postman, for example, suggests that written language has lost all utility as a medium of communication. Nevertheless, he entrusts his own messages to print and obviously expects someone to read them. He asserts that "an important function of teaching reading is to make students accessible to political and historical myth," without noting that reading might also provide grounds for rejecting such myth. One inestimable advantage of writing is that it forces the writer to make *statements* which can then be examined, analyzed, and even evaluated. Criticism is inherently a literary mode. It may be true, though I would dispute it, that written language appeals more to reason than to the emotions, but is this an argument against reading (any more than the opposite is an argument for or against electronic media)?

The fact that relatively few people may currently take advantage of reading seems to me irrelevant. It is almost certainly a consequence of the way reading is taught. There is information and knowledge and pleasure in print—not just in novels, but in newspapers, magazines, comics, programs, menus, directories, scripts, scenarios, letters, notices, and graffiti. Even Postman would include books in his brave new resource centers, despite his uncertainty about who might read them. He even suggests that being able to read might somehow be degrading, that it makes the individual a tool of his government or of any bureaucrat. But is illiteracy any better? Once again, I think he confuses the act of reading with the consequences of the way we teach it. The price of literacy need not be the reader's free will and intelligence.

Postman further argues that written language has been misused and worn out, that the world is full of written garbage. But people need not read everything that has been written; one advantage of being able to read is that you can be selective. It may be true that reprints of Postman's paper will help to clutter thousands of useless filing cabinets, never to be looked at again. But one of the more dubious benefits of the electronic revolution is that neither the spoken word nor the visual gesture will remain biodegradable in the future. Students armed with cassette recorders and video cameras will record every cough and scratch. If ever there were media that inundated themselves the moment they were created, they are audiotaping and videotaping, open invitations to capture the trivial for posterity. One advantage of old-fashioned manual media like writing and painting is that they require *effort*; squirting a video camera at "life" is an indiscriminate way of being creative.

It is a fallacy to assume that anything written language can do videotape can do better. There is good and bad grammar in film just as in written language, and there is at least as much ignorance about film. It is fallacious to believe that either film or television gives more information than writing. *Different media do not convey the same information about the same event,* but offer different perspectives (Olson, 1974).

All media are selective; you take your choice whether you see an event through the eye of the writer or of the camera operator. One beauty of written language is the manner in which it is selective. We tend to overlook how much information words give us about context, about what is said "between the lines." Words give more information than pictures because they can take so much account of what the reader already knows. When I view a documentary, I need a spoken or written commentary to tell me what I should be looking at and how to relate it to what I know.

Any notion that film provides a particularly veridical or unadulterated image of "life" or "experience" is naive. Where does the "creativity" come in? Reading about a good meal does not reduce hunger, but neither does a picture of it. Movies do not automatically enhance our experience, whether of the Vietnam conflict or of sex. A competent writer may give a reasonable impression of what it is like to eat a gourmet meal, suffer a napalm attack, or make love, while an incompetent movie producer might do little more than illustrate the movements involved. (Will electronic exercises teach children that the art of any medium is to use the receiver's imagination?) Vietnam was the world's most televised war, but "bringing it into the living room" did not seem to end it any sooner. Could the fact that there was little written literature on Vietnam—as opposed to "factual reporting"—have anything to do with the way the war was tolerated, regardless of demonstrations, which were themselves televised into visual tedium?

Postman admits that nobody knows what the consequence would be of turning schools into electronic circuses. He does not mention that the experiment has already been tried to a certain extent and has failed. During the past decade, most new and many old facilities in schools and universities were decked out with audiovisual novelties, much of the equipment never used and now being taken out. And just as much ignorance is being displayed in dismantling the electronic sideshows as was involved in their establishment. Hard-core ignorance is not exclusive to written-language experts.

As Postman implies, we have scarcely any idea today of what schools are for. We do not know what we should do in schools. We do not even understand what we are doing in schools. Ignorance abounds. Not only do we not understand why hundreds of thousands of children fail to learn to read each year, but also we have no idea what happens with the hundreds of thousands of children who succeed. Practically everything we try to teach in educational institutions we teach ineptly. If we succeed at all, it can be reasonably predicted that the student will not want to practice what he or she has learned or will do so reluctantly. And there is absolutely no evidence that we will do any better if we encourage our students to film and tape-record everything in sight.

Master teachers, love of learning, respect for knowledge, or academic integrity—these are more than exceptions within the modern system; they are aberrations. Schools are training institutions, managed by teachers who are themselves taught in training institutions, and the entire perverse and misbegotten process is founded on the premise that no one should actually think. *That* is the political issue.

The prime concern of schools is getting through the day. Schools are not concerned with literacy, nor with creativity, nor with intelligence, except as items on tests or in end-of-term reports. Superintendents and trustees are concerned with buildings, budgets, and enrollment projections. Principals are concerned with pacification, keeping the lid on, and maintaining stability. And teachers are concerned with discipline and control; how could they be otherwise, since thinking is an individual activity that produces unmanageable oddballs, whether in the classroom or in the staff room? At every level there is only one concern, it involves neither "learning" nor the child; it is good administration. I know there are exceptions, but the discussion is not about exceptions, nor can most school systems tolerate them.

Schools make a poor job of teaching reading, suggests Postman, so why not release teachers from that burden and entrust them instead with something important, something "relevant," like "helping young people to resolve some of their more wrenching emotional problems?" One can only wonder how anyone could think it is only literacy that schools can foul up. Will teachers be good for anything except distributing popcorn if we make them ushers in an electric circus?

The Alternative to Ignorance

The opposite of ignorance is not knowledge, which is either a dead end or a route to new ignorance. The opposite of ignorance is understanding, achieved only through active awareness and thought. And awareness and thought are not faculties that you acquire from experts or skills that can be taught in schools. Rather, they are aspects of human nature that are inherent in all children, until they are drilled out of them by a process that is called socialization.

The opposite of ignorance is keeping the mind alive, always considering alternatives, never shutting the system down. It is remembering that every question might be put differently, that authority is not necessarily right, and that superficial glibness (including this paper and Postman's) is not necessarily erudition. The opposite of ignorance is never to rest content doing something you do not understand.

I am not arguing for the unattainable. Being told what to do is a good short-run solution in an emergency situation, such as changing a tire or floating off the roof in a flood. But education should not be an emergency situation, and even if no one is really sure of what is going on in the classroom, at least the question could be mutually examined by those who are most involved, the child and the teacher.

I am not proposing that the printed word should remain the keystone of education, an extreme as radical as Postman's nomination of electronic media as a substitute. I would much prefer not to make a big issue of reading instruction or of anything else. In fact, I would suggest that we forget about "teaching" for a while, or at least have a moratorium on the topic, and instead think a little about how schools might be reorganized as places where children and adults collaboratively or independently learn, a situation that would guarantee the exercise of thought. A prime focus for initial study might be how the acquisition of literacy in written language and electronic media might help the individual teacher or child to resist the blandishments and misinformation that daily assault all our senses. But there is much ignorance for us to think our way out of in these topics.

Let me go out even further on my self-appointed limb. Children do not learn by instruction; they learn by example, and they learn by making sense of what are essentially meaningful situations. Children have been learning since birth. They learn when they hear adults talking to them or to each other. They learn when a parent lets them take a chance with a hammer and nails. They learn when they find it necessary to check the price of sports equipment in a catalog. Always they learn in order to make sense of something and especially when there is an example, a model, to be copied. Even when they learn to loot stores, sniff glue, or mug cripples, they do so by example and because it makes sense in their environment. If thinking or asking questions seemed to pay off, and if some good models were around, children might even spend a few years at school doing just that—thinking and asking questions.

Encouraging people to think is an enormously political issue. It is not one that currently occupies much of the attention of politicians, nor is it a dominant question in schools. In educational psychology, thinking is usually equated with problem solving, concept formation, and excursions to the nearest museum. The alternative to ignorance would be revolutionary in more than one sense of the word. It might even enable us to start asking the right sorts of questions about education.

Eradicating ignorance might also put a lot of experts out of business. What will be the use of having all the right answers, even electronic ones, if people are going to start asking different kinds of questions and, worse still, to start educating their children to do the same?

2
Twelve Easy Ways to Make Learning to Read Difficult[*]

[*]and One Difficult Way to Make it Easy

I have collected a dozen precepts on the topic of how to teach reading. The list is set out, concisely tabulated in a form suitable for framing, in the table below. I make no claim to originality

---

Twelve Rules for Reading Teachers

1. Aim for early mastery of the rules of reading.
2. Ensure that phonic skills are learned and used.
3. Teach letters or words one at a time, making sure each new letter or word is learned before moving on.
4. Make word-perfect reading the prime objective.
5. Discourage guessing; be sure children read carefully.
6. Insist upon accuracy.
7. Provide immediate feedback.
8. Detect and correct inappropriate eye movements.
9. Identify and give special attention to problem readers as soon as possible.
10. Make sure children understand the importance of reading and the seriousness of falling behind.
11. Take the opportunity during reading instruction to improve spelling and written expression, and also insist on the best possible spoken English.
12. If the method you are using is unsatisfactory, try another. Always be alert for new materials and techniques.

Reprinted with permission from Frank Smith (Ed.), *Psycholinguistics and Reading*. New York: Holt, Rinehart and Winston, 1973.

for my specimens. In fact, I have chosen them because they have such widespread currency; they are part of the conventional wisdom. They might not be considered out of place displayed on the staff room wall as a model of exemplary practice, or enshrined in the pages of manuals for teachers (which is where I found most of them in the first place).

Some of my twelve precepts are venerable to the point of senility. I shall examine them one by one, and indicate why each in its own way may be regarded as a potential and powerful method of interfering in the process of learning to read.

1. Aim for Early Mastery of the Rules of Reading

This rule is absurd because there are no rules of reading, at least none that can be specified with sufficient precision to teach a child. All proficient readers have acquired an implicit knowledge of how to read, but this knowledge has been developed through the practice of reading, not through anything that is taught in school. The learning process is identical with that by which infants develop a set of internal rules for producing and comprehending spoken language without the benefit of any formal instruction. And just as no linguist is able to formulate a complete and adequate set of grammatical rules that could be used to program a computer (or a child) to use spoken language, so no theorist has yet achieved anything like an adequate insight into the knowledge that people acquire and use when they become fluent readers.

But even if we did have a clearer understanding of the reading process, it would be doubtful whether anyone should try to give this understanding directly to children. After all, millions of children have learned to read in the past without any profound insight on the part of their instructors into what the children were learning to do. There is absolutely no evidence that teaching grammar helps a child to learn to speak, and none that drills in phonics or other nonreading activities help the development of reading. It is not difficult to argue that mastery of phonics develops only to the extent that reading proficiency is acquired, just as grammar is a meaningful and useful subject (if at all) only to those who already know how to use language.

Typically, what are called "rules of reading" are hints or slogans for reading instruction. Learning to read is not a matter of mastering rules. Children learn to read by reading.

2. Ensure that Phonic Skills Are Learned and Used

A prominent aspect of the "reading by rules" fallacy is the notion that reading ability depends on a knowledge of spelling-to-sound correspondences. (In its less sophisticated form, this notion merely asserts that children must learn the "sounds of letters" without any realization of just how complex and unpredictable spelling-to-sound correspondences are.) But reading is not accomplished by decoding to sound; meaning must usually be grasped before the appropriate sounds can be produced, and the production of sounds alone does not give meaning. Decoding directly from letters to sound is unnecessary as well as inefficient.

It quickly becomes obvious to anyone who gives more than passing attention to the actual process of reading that fluent readers do not translate written symbols into sound in order to understand what they are reading. Nevertheless, it is frequently argued that a mastery of phonics must surely be essential for children; otherwise, how would they ever learn to recognize words that they had not met in print before, words that are not in their "sight vocabulary?" There are two good reasons why the last resort of a child in such circumstances should be to turn to phonics.

The first objection to phonics as a way of reading is that it is conspicuously unreliable and cumbersome. Studies at the Southwest Regional Laboratory for Educational Development showed that 166 rules would be required to account for the most frequent correspondences in just 6000 one- and two-syllable words in the vocabulary of 6- to 9-year-olds—and these 166 rules would still not account for over 10 percent of the most common words which would have to be excluded as "exceptions." There is no rule for predicting which of many alternative rules should apply on any particular occasion, any more than there are rules for determining which words are exceptions. The rules often cannot be applied unless one is aware of the meaning and syntactic role of the word and the way it carries stress. In other words, phonics is easy provided one knows what a word is in the first place.

The very complexity and indeterminacy of such a system makes it remarkable that anyone should expect children ever to try to learn it. Nevertheless, many educators believe that teaching at least an arbitrary part of the system is the answer to "the reading problem." But even if children were gifted and gullible enough to learn such a system, there is absolutely no evidence that they could ever actually use it in the process of reading. Quite the reverse, it is easy to show that any attempt to read by translating letters to sounds through the application and integration of phonic rules could result only in catastrophic overloading of short-term memory. Besides, the use of spelling-to-sound rules to identify words is as absurd as clipping a lawn with nail scissors. Far more efficient and economical alternatives are available.

This leads to the second objection to the phonics fallacy, namely that sounding out words letter by letter (or the even more complicated task of identifying and articulating "letter clusters") is the last resort of the fluent reader, a fact already known by most children whose natural perception of reading has not been distorted in the process of reading instruction.

3. Teach Letters or Words One at a Time, Making Sure Each New Letter or Word Is Learned Before Moving On

There is a widespread misconception that many children have trouble learning the names of objects and words and letters, and that only constant repetition will help to fix a name in a child's mind. This view is based on an oversimplification of learning. There are two quite distinct aspects of any name-learning task, the first being to discover how to differentiate the named object or type of object from all other objects—which is essentially a concept formation problem—and the second to discover and associate that concept with its name. By far the more difficult of the two parts of the task is the first—discovering the rules that differentiate categories. Name-associating itself seems so easy as to be almost trivial. Children in the first 6 years of life learn perhaps a dozen new words, most of them "names," every day, often in a single trial (Miller, 1977).

The manner in which children learn how to define the category to which a name belongs is instructive. They look at the situation in which the name seems to be applied and try to extract some features that will mark the situation so that they will recognize it in the future. They look for, but do not ask to be told, some *rules* that will specify the defining characteristics of the category. They construct "hypotheses" about what the concept is. We can get an idea of what these hypotheses are by looking at the errors that children make. If, for example, they call all and only four-legged animals "dog," then we may conclude that their current hypothesis is that "dog" simply means four-legged animals. If they apply the name to four-legged animals and tables, we can assume that animation is not one of their hypotheses. If they call only their own dogs "dog," they are undergeneralizing.

Children can generate hypotheses only by comparing examples of the category being named with nonexamples of the same category. It is as important to be aware of four-legged animals that are not called "dog" as to see some others that are. Children can modify their hypotheses only by testing them and receiving feedback. They learn practically nothing if they are simply shown a dog and told "That is a dog," except perhaps that a category named "dog" exists. They learn only when they can compare what is a dog with other objects that (to them) might be but are not dogs. More specifically, they learn when they discover that objects that they would not call "dog" (according to their hypotheses) are in fact dogs, and that objects that they would call "dog" (according to their hypotheses) are in fact not dogs.

A similar situation applies when children approach the task of learning the names of letters or words. Simply to be shown the letter *H* over and over again, while being told "This is an 'h,'" is not going to help them discover what *H* is. They are still quite likely to call a *K* "h" and perhaps *H* "k." Instead they must find out how *H* and *K* are different, which means first that they must see them together (or at least have a chance to hypothesize what makes *H* different from *K*) and second have a chance to test their hypotheses about the difference between the two.

The manner in which letter and word names are learned is just one of several critical issues involved in understanding the task confronting children when they learn to read. Learning to distinguish among letters and words is an obvious case in which there are "rules" to be learned in reading, but these are not rules that we can teach. They are like the rules we learn for distinguishing cats and dogs or for spoken language—rules that we have acquired without instruction and cannot talk about. Instead children learn by being given the evidence, positive and negative, and also the opportunity to test their theories for themselves.

4. Make Word-Perfect Reading the Prime Objective

There is another reason why emphasis should not be put on the learning or identification of words in isolation, and this is that it is the most difficult way to do it. All fluent readers use other cues when they are required to read letters or words. It is much easier to identify a letter when it occurs in a word, or a word when it appears in a meaningful sentence, than when it is standing alone. As I have already pointed out, the identification of individual words is not the most important part of reading. Far more visual information is required to identify words standing alone (or as if they were standing alone) than to identify words in a sentence. Because of the information-processing limitations of our visual system and working memory, it is the handling of large amounts of visual information that makes reading difficult. One of the most important parts of learning to read is learning to use as little visual information as possible.

Fluent readers do not read words, they read meanings. Reading for meaning is far easier than reading words. Children seem to know this instinctively, no doubt because of the strain that reading every word puts on their information-processing capacities.

5. Discourage Guessing; Be Sure Children Read Carefully

I have already referred to the role of hypotheses in the identification of unfamiliar words. I have also referred to the need to spend as little time as possible lingering over every word. Efficient readers make maximum use of a minimum of visual information. Reading for meaning is easier than reading for words. There is another critical factor that I have not yet mentioned: reading quickly is easier than reading slowly. What all the preceding distills down to is that "reading carefully" is not efficient reading, and reading without anticipating is not reading at all. Goodman (1970) has aptly termed reading "a psycholinguistic guessing game." In order to read, one must predict, not recklessly but on an informed basis. Informed guessing means making the best use of nonvisual information, of what one already knows. More precisely, in order to read one must constantly form expectations that reduce the uncertainty of what one is reading, and therefore reduce the amount of visual information required to extract its meaning (see chapter 3).

We all know that when reading an unfamiliar or difficult text, whether a complex novel, a technical article, or something in a fairly unfamiliar foreign language, it is impossible to read and simultaneously refer to a dictionary, or to slog through the text a sentence at a time. We may be tempted to slow down, but the only efficient strategy is, in fact, to speed up, to read on. When it is necessary to "read carefully" for one reason or another, we do not try to do it cold. Instead we take a quick scan through the material "to see what it is about"—which means to get the essence of the meaning—and then read through a second time, still relatively fast, to get the details.

An important generalization reveals itself through a number of the observations that I have made so far—that *reading provides its own cues*. The best way to discover the meaning of a difficult passage is to read more of the passage. The best way to identify an unfamiliar word in text is to draw inferences from the rest of the text. The best way to learn the strategies and models for identifying new words "by analogy" is to read. Any instructional method that interferes with reading must almost certainly interfere with learning to read.

6. Insist Upon Accuracy

Learning cannot take place without error. We cannot learn to use names correctly, for animals, letters, or words, unless we accept the possibility of being "wrong." Children must take the risk of using a word incorrectly in order to find out whether the rules they have for identifying or using that word are correct; they must use their rules in order to get feedback. I have also argued that reading is highly dependent on guessing and that reading for meaning is both far easier and far more important than reading to identify words. Again it is obvious that children must be prepared to make errors; in fact, one of the greatest difficulties that a child can face in the process of learning to read is to be inhibited from responding because of the risk of being wrong.

There is no need for scientific evidence to demonstrate that learning is not possible unless we accept the chance of being wrong. If children know they are right before saying something, then the feedback that they are in fact right provides them with no information at all; they already know they were right. But if children make a response, if they name an object or venture an opinion about meaning, knowing that it is possible they might be wrong, then they will learn something whatever the outcome. If they happen to be "right," then they have confirmed their existing hypotheses. If they happen to be "wrong," then they have acquired some equally important information; they have learned that they must modify their hypotheses. That is the way children naturally try to learn—by testing hypotheses—provided, of course, that they have not been taught that society places a high premium on being right and that it is better to stay quiet than to be wrong. Adults who treat, or who encourage other children to treat, misreadings as stupidities, jokes, or transgressions do more than misperceive the basic nature of reading; they also block the principal way in which reading is learned.

7. Provide Immediate Feedback

Both good and poor beginning readers make errors, but they differ in the type of errors that they make. One difference between the good beginning reader and the one heading for trouble lies in the overreliance on visual information that inefficient, or improperly taught, beginning readers tend to show, at the expense of sense. The words they read may not make sense, but they look pretty much like the words on the page. The good reader, on the other hand, will get the sense of the passage but may omit, insert, or change a number of words. It is clear that the better readers barely look at the individual words on the page;

they minimize their use of visual information. The problem for the teacher is to distinguish between the two types of reader. It is easy enough for the teacher (or other children in the class) to jump on a child and give immediate feedback if a word is read incorrectly, but this feedback has no relevance if the child is not reading to identify words in the first place, but reading for meaning.

"Immediate feedback" is a dangerous rule to apply indiscriminately. It is necessary to know what feedback is being given for. Feedback implies answering a specific question. If the child is in fact practising individual word identification and wants to know "Is this word 'elephant'?" then immediate feedback may help (with a qualification that I shall mention in a moment). But if the child is reading to get the general meaning—which means reading fluently—then immediate feedback on words is more than just misplaced or irrelevant; it is disruptive.

There is a second important difference concerning the errors of good and poor beginning readers. Even good readers make occasional errors of meaning; they read anomalously. But a difference lies in what happens at the end of the sentence or passage, at the point where the anomaly should become apparent. Better readers will go back and self-correct; they have been paying attention to the meaning of what they read. But word-by-word readers will have no reason to go back and self-correct even if they have been producing absolute nonsense. They were not reading for meaning in the first place. There is a simple strategy, then, for distinguishing children who are reading for meaning from the others. Wait and see if they self-correct errors of meaning. Of course, the teacher who pounces on every misread word as soon as it is uttered will not have the opportunity of finding that out.

The preceding discussion leads to a second important generalization, that *reading provides its own feedback*. Provided we read for meaning, we can always check whether errors of interpretation, and even of word identification, have occurred.

8. Detect and Correct Inappropriate Eye Movements

An inappropriate eye movement means the reader is looking in the wrong place. This rarely occurs because there is something wrong with the reader's eyes, but rather because the reader does not know what to look for. Unless a child has a gross visual deficiency that manifests itself outside reading, there is little justification for blaming reading difficulties on visual defects or bad habits. Any child who can recognize a character on a television screen or spear a pea on a plate has the visual acuity and control necessary to be able to read. But that does not mean the child will know where to look. Knowing where to look depends on the nonvisual skills of reading. Drilling the eyes to move blindly from one meaningless position to another is a pointless exercise.

9. Identify and Give Special Attention to Problem Readers as Soon as Possible

Very often far too much is required of early readers; they are expected to demonstrate skills beyond the capacity of fluent adult readers. Relevant examples that I have already mentioned concern the identification of unfamiliar words on the basis of spelling-to-sound rules alone and the requirement that reading aloud should be word-perfect. A third factor lies in the type of material children often are expected to read. Many primers bear absolutely no relevance to a child's particular life or language, and short sentences barely connected by a story line place a premium on word identification and provide little support for intelligent guessing. Subject matter texts that children are later expected to comprehend and appreciate often present an even worse obstacle. Teachers and other adults frequently expect children to read and learn from "resource material" so opaque and dull that it is doubtful whether the adults themselves could bear to read it, let alone learn from it. Furthermore, expectations about comprehension itself are far too high to be realistic. The proper distinction is not drawn between *understanding* what a sentence or passage or book is about, which means grasping the author's meaning, and *recall* of what was said, which is quite a different matter. While recall and understanding are related, in the sense that the former can rarely occur in the absence of the latter, committing detailed information to memory and retrieving it on a later occasion is a complex cognitive task that depends on much more than mere reading ability. There are very stringent limits on how much information can be put into long-term memory at any one time. In fact the requirement that a reader try to store in memory an unreasonably large amount of the information in a passage is a sure way to interfere with the process of reading altogether.

I mention the preceding points because there is a risk that children will be classified as reading problems when the only problem that exists lies in the unreasonable expectations of a parent or teacher, or of the system in which the teacher and child interact. Sometimes the problem lies in a complete misunderstanding of what constitutes good reading: "Johnny is above average at comprehension but he persists in making careless errors with individual words." Reading and diagnostic tests are a very poor guide to reading ability in this respect. The materials and methods used to "measure" reading in fact only measure what can be measured—facility in an assortment of drills, rules, and "power" tasks that at best bear only a tangential relation to fluent reading.

Treating a child as a "special case" always carries a number of unpleasant side effects, particularly damaging in the case of reading. Being singled out all too often adds to a child's anxiety, increases tension, and leads to concentration on detail and even more apprehension about errors. Involvement with clinics and consultants scarcely contributes to the confidence required to read with the flexibility that makes comprehension possible. And if children continue to fall short of expectations despite the special attention they get when identified as a "problem," then the only way they can go is in the direction of further confusion, ultimately with the risk of being labelled minimally brain-damaged (which means "We really cannot understand why he does not benefit from our instruction").

I do not want to dwell on the moral, social, or personal implications of acting rashly in labelling a child as inadequate. But there is one practical consideration that should be taken into account. The remedial measures taken when children are identified as having a reading problem frequently result in their reading less than before. They spend more time on exercises, drills, tests, and interviews; more time trying to boost "conceptual skills" and general language ability (and even pronunciation) and less time actually reading. The difficulty before the "problem" was identified might well have been that the child was not doing enough reading in order to learn to read, yet the "cure" turns out to be even less reading experience.

10. Make Sure Children Understand the Importance of Reading and the Seriousness of Falling Behind

The only way to learn to read is with confidence and enjoyment. Once again I make the point not as a moral judgment but for purely practical reasons. Anything that makes reading difficult, or unpleasant, or threatening, makes learning to read more difficult. Lack of confidence, unwillingness to risk errors, and a reluctance to become *involved* in reading will all contribute to making learning to read impossible.

There is nothing reprehensible in falling behind one's classmates in reading instruction, and absolutely no damage can be done, except in terms of the school schedule and the expectations (and sometimes the egos) of adults. Reading is not learned competitively, and no convincing evidence exists that there is a critical age for learning to read. The most that can be said about a 7-year-old who is a year behind is that he reads like an average 6-year-old. This 1-year lag may be disconcerting for parents and teacher, but there is no sound psychological reason why it should be regarded as a precursor of educational catastrophe for the child. The notion is absurd that because 20 percent of a class of children read less fluently than the other 80 percent, remedial action should abolish the bottom 20 percent. The aim should obviously be that all children progress toward fluent reading, not that they should change place in relative ranks.

As I have indicated, tests are poor indicators of reading ability, partly because they are limited in what they measure, but largely because they are almost invariably based on a total misunderstanding of what reading involves. (My precepts 1, 2, 4, 5, 6, and perhaps 11 could be interpreted as a large part of the test-maker's creed.) The purpose of reading is not to score high on reading tests, and progress in learning to read does not require keeping up with the neighbors.

11. Take the Opportunity During Reading Instruction to Improve Spelling and Written Expression, and Also Insist on the Best Possible Spoken English

Writing and reading involve several different systems of knowledge and skill. Knowledge of spelling is never used in the process of identifying a word, and words are frequently read for which the spelling is not known. (For this reason, the visual knowledge of how words should look may be used to test whether a written word has been spelled correctly.) Reading assists writing, but not vice versa. Apart from anything else, writing is too slow to do anything but interfere with the process of reading, just as the mechanics of the writing act can interfere chronically with children's expression of their thought. Even so, instruction in written language which aims at getting well-articulated thoughts onto paper very often finds itself more concerned with such disruptive side issues as "correct" spelling and grammar, formalized layout, page and paragraph numeration, and neatness. But the analogies between the disruptive precepts of "good reading instruction" and those of "good writing instruction" are too extensive to pursue here.

I am not saying that the obvious relations between reading and writing should be concealed, but only that the fragile process of learning to read—of achieving that delicate balance between fidelity to the printed page and overcoming the strain that an overload of visual information places on eye and brain—should not be further complicated by introducing worries about handwriting or spelling.

Similarly, spoken English is largely irrelevant to reading. There can only be interference with learning to read if children must worry about how to pronounce what they read—literally a superficial aspect of reading. Children who read *I do not have any candy* as "I don't have no candy" have picked up all the significant features of meaning from the text and succeeded in translating them into their own thought and language. Expecting them to read word-perfectly not only confuses pedantry with reading, but also it will probably convey to children a completely distorted notion of what reading is. They may be deluded into requiring far more visual information from the text than any mature reader would be able to cope with.

One of the great advantages of conventional English spelling is that it appears to be maximally efficient for all dialects (Chomsky and Halle, 1968). The particular dialect that a child speaks makes no intrinsic difference to the basic task of learning to read. Printed materials are rarely anyone's spoken language written down. Of course, discrepancies among dialects may lead to communication and even sociocultural conflicts within the classroom, especially if the teacher expects the child to read word for word (which even the teacher would probably find difficult to do) or if every reading lesson is used as an occasion for undermining a child's native spoken language expression.

12. If the Method You Are Using Is Unsatisfactory, Try Another. Always Be Alert for New Materials and Techniques

The belief that improvement in reading instruction lies just around the corner in the form of another kit of drills, some new basal readers, or a cabinet of technological trickery, is based on an egregious educational fallacy. The belief rests upon the naive assumption that an ideal method of teaching reading exists for every child and that all a teacher need do is find the right method or wait for the educational industry to provide it—together, of course, with the infallible "test" that will match every child with the best method.

There are trivial but quite valid objections to any random, trial-and-error, hit-or-miss imposition of materials in the hope that one will brush the child with the magical dust of reading.

There is no guarantee that any method will be an improvement on the one before, and there is no test, no set of evaluation procedures, to help teachers make reliable choices. We tend to overlook the damage and despair that constant exposure to different instructional methods, and repeated failure, can produce in a child. We tend to forget that many millions of children learned to read without the benefit of the techniques and technology we have today, let alone those we hope to have tomorrow. Many children have learned in classrooms at least as large as those around today, with desks nailed down in rows, and using abysmally printed and sanctimoniously written material. Rather than devote so much time—and sanguine hope—to how children will learn to read in the great new days of the future, it would be more instructive to examine how children learned to read in the bad old days of the past.

A more serious objection to dependence on methods and materials than the fact that it is unrealistic is that it reflects a totally distorted view of what is required to improve the quality of instruction. The focus is all wrong; it should be on the child, not on the instructional materials. In fact the common critical inadequacy of all my twelve precepts is that they fail to take any account of the child's point of view. They are all directed to the question of what the teacher ought to do, not what the child might be trying to do.

I hope to make my point clearer as I turn from the negative and attempt to summarize in a positive way the alternative I have to offer, difficult though I promise it will be.

One Difficult Rule for making Learning to Read Easy

I shall introduce a brief transitional stage in my progression from the easy to the difficult. I offer a guideline, a bridge to my one rule for making learning to read easy. The guideline is this: *The only way to make learning to read easy is to make reading easy.* My guideline may appear banal to the point of meaninglessness but it must be justified before I go on to the difficult rule, which otherwise might appear even more pointless.

Learning to read is a complex and delicate task in which almost all the rules, all the cues, and all the feedback can be obtained only through the act of reading itself. Children learn to read only by reading. Therefore, the only way to facilitate their learning to read is to make reading easy for them. This means continuously making critical and insightful decisions—not forcing children to read for words when they are, or should be, reading for meaning; not forcing them to slow down when they should speed up; not requiring caution when they should be taking chances; not worrying about speech when the topic is reading; not discouraging errors. . . .

But I do not intend to offer a collection of proscriptions in exchange for the prescriptions that I have so destructively criticized. The simple point is that the twelve easy rules all make reading more difficult, and reading is a difficult enough task already. The twelve golden rules are dross.

The skill of riding a bicycle comes with riding a bicycle. We do not offer children lectures, diagrams, and drills on the component skills of bicycle riding. We sit them on the saddle and use a guiding hand or training wheels to make sure they do not fall off while they teach themselves the precarious art of keeping balance. Forcing them to worry about laws of motion and centers of gravity would obviously confuse them.

Making learning to read easy means ensuring cues at the time a child needs them, ensuring feedback of the kind required at the time it is required, providing encouragement when it is sought. Making learning to read easy requires an understanding of the reading process and of what the child is trying to do.

Now I have reached my one difficult rule, the antithesis of the twelve easy ways: *Respond to what the child is trying to do.* To my mind, this rule is basic. There is no alternative. The rule recognizes that the motivation and direction of learning to read can only come from the child and that learners must look for the knowledge and skills they need only in the process of reading. Learning to read is a problem for the child to solve. Glance back at all my twelve easy rules and you will see that none of them is really concerned with what the child is doing—at the most only with what a remote authority suggests the child should be doing.

Obviously, my one rule is difficult. It requires insight, tolerance, sensitivity, and patience; it demands an understanding of the nature of reading, a rejection of formulae, less reliance on tests, and more receptivity to the child. Its main demand is a total rejection of the ethos of our day—that the answer to all our problems lies in improved method and technology—and of the emphasis on method that pervades almost all of teacher-training.

The last thing I want to do is imply that teachers have been doing everything wrong. Quite the reverse, my interest is in the fact that for so long, with so many children, teachers have been doing things that are obviously right.

Nothing I have said can change the world as it was yesterday. Any method, any approach to reading instruction, that worked before this essay was written is obviously still going to work after it has been subjected to a critical review. Yesterday's methods might even work a little better if we get some insight into what really made them effective.

Most teachers are eclectic; they do not act as brainless purveyors of predigested instruction. (That is why there is the frightening trend these days to produce "teacher-proof" materials.) In short, teachers—at least the best of them—are good intuitively. They are effective without knowing why. The word *intuitive* may sound vague and unscientific; it is a word that is widely discredited, but mainly I think because the quality of intuition is not well understood. Here is an off-the-cuff definition of *intuition*: a responsiveness to the intangible forces and motivations that largely determine the manifest nature of events. Put in psycholinguistic terms, intuition implies access to underlying structure without awareness of the grammar relating this structure to the physical events that impinge directly upon our senses. More colloquially, intuition is a feel for what is really going on. In terms of reading instruction, intuition is a sensitivity for the unspoken intellectual demands of a child, encouraging and responding to hypothesis-testing.

The good intuitive teacher, in other words, is one who instinctively ignores the twelve easy rules.

3
The Role of Prediction in Reading

A growing number of analyses of reading are playing particular attention to the use that readers must make of prior knowledge relevant to the material they are endeavoring to read (e.g., Goodman, 1968, 1970; Hochberg, 1970; Kolers, 1970; Smith, 1971, 1973). In formal psychological jargon this use of prior knowledge is frequently referred to as *hypothesis-testing*; teachers know it more familiarly as *guessing*; and I shall refer to it as *prediction*. Reading is impossible without prediction, and since it is only through reading that children learn to read, it follows that the opportunity to develop and employ skills of prediction must be a critical part of learning to read.

It is not necessary, however, that prediction be taught, for prediction is as much a part of spoken language comprehension as it is of reading. Children with sufficient verbal ability to understand written material that is read to them have both the competence and the experience to direct their ability in prediction to reading. My aim is to demonstrate that prediction is essential for reading, that everyone who can comprehend spoken language is capable of prediction, and that prediction is routinely practised in reading by beginners as well as by fluent readers.

Four Reasons for Prediction

1. Individual words have too many meanings. Words in our language tend to be multiply ambiguous (like the word *multiply* in this sentence), and the most common words have the most meanings (Fries, 1940). Everyday words like *come, go, have, take, table,* and *chair* not only have a multiplicity of different meanings, but they are often also ambiguous as to their grammatical function. How is the word *house* pronounced? The word cannot even be articulated until the reader knows whether it is a noun or a verb. Among the most frequently used words of English, prepositions have so many different meanings they take up more space in dictionaries than words in any other syntactic class. It should be noted, however, that speakers and writers are almost never aware of this potential ambiguity and that listeners and readers are rarely aware of the multiplicity of possible meanings either.

2. The spellings of words do not indicate how they should be pronounced. There are over 300 "spelling-to-sound correspon-

Reprinted with permission from *Elementary English* 52(3):305–311, 1975.

dence rules" of English (Venezky, 1967), and there is no rule that will specify when any of these particular rules must apply or when the spelling to be "sounded out" is an exception. The rules of phonics are highly complex. To take a very simple example, how should a word beginning with *ho* be pronounced? The answer depends on whether the *ho* is followed by *..t*, *..ot*, *..ok*, *..rizon*, *..use*, *..rse*, *..pe*, *..ney*, *..ist*, *..ur*, or *..nest*, eleven different possibilities (all depending on what follows the initial letters, indicating that phonics must be applied from right to left).

3. There is a limit to how much of the "visual information" of print the brain can process during reading. Flash a line of about thirty random letters on a screen for about a tenth of a second and the most an experienced reader will be able to recognize is four or five letters. This four-letter or five-letter limit in fact represents an entire second that it takes the brain to decide what these five letters are; it is not possible for anything else to be seen. The condition can be characterized as one of "tunnel vision." In other words, for as long as one is trying to identify letters one after the other, reading is an impossibly slow and restricted process (Smith and Holmes, 1971).

4. The capacity of short-term memory (or "working memory") is limited (Atkinson and Shiffrin, 1970; Simon, 1974). Not more than six or seven unrelated items—say an unfamiliar telephone number—can be held in short-term memory at any one time. Try to overload an already filled short-term memory and other information will be lost. As a consequence, it is virtually impossible to read a word more than four or five letters long a letter at a time. By the time the end is reached, the beginning will be forgotten. It is similarly impossible to store the first words of a sentence while waiting to get to its end before making a decision about meaning. By the time the end of the sentence is reached, the beginning will have been forgotten.

Defining Prediction

There is a common feature underlying the four reasons for prediction that have just been listed. In each case the brain is confronted by too many possibilities; it must decide among more alternatives than it can handle. Decision-making takes time, and there is a fundamental rule that applies to every aspect of decision-making, whether it involves the identification of a single letter or word in a line of type or the comprehension of a sentence or an entire book. The fundamental rule is this: The greater the number of alternatives, the more time is required for a decision (Garner, 1962). Recognition is never instantaneous. We may be able to identify a letter or a word if it comes from a small set of known alternatives—when we know in advance that it is a vowel, or the name of a flower—but the same letter or word can be quite unrecognizable if it comes from a larger set of alternatives. The reason for this bottleneck is simple: the greater the number of possible alternatives, the more information the brain has to process in order to reach a decision. The art of fluent reading lies in the skilled reduction of the amount of visual information the brain has to process. If you know a letter will be either *A* or *B*, you need only a glimpse of that letter to decide which it is. But if the letter could be any one of the twenty-six letters of the alphabet, much more visual information will have to be taken into account.

My general definition of *prediction* is "the prior elimination of unlikely alternatives." In the jargon of information theory, prediction is the reduction of uncertainty. The qualification "unlikely" in the preceding definition must be emphasized. *Prediction* in the sense in which I am using the word does not mean wild guessing, nor does it mean staking everything on a simple outcome. Rather, *prediction* means the elimination from contention of those possibilities that are highly unlikely and the examination first of those possibilities that are most likely. Such a procedure is highly efficient for making decisions involving language.

Prediction in Operation

Imagine that I have written twenty-six letters of the alphabet on twenty-six index cards, one letter to each card, and that I shuffle the pack of cards, select one at random, and ask you to guess what that card is. You could very rightly object that since every letter is equally probable, nothing you know could in any way increase your chances of making a correct guess. Whatever letter you might choose to guess, the probability that you will be correct is exactly the same, namely, one in twenty-six.

However, letters do not occur randomly in the English language. Some have a much higher probability of occurrence than others; for example, the most common letter, *E*, is forty times more likely than the least common letter, *Z*. If I asked you to guess the seventeenth letter of the fifth line of the twenty-third page of a random sample of 1000 books in any library, you would be correct forty times more often if you guessed *E* every time than if you consistently guessed *Z*. So when a letter is selected at random from English text, your prior knowledge of the language can obviously make a difference to your chances of making a correct guess.

It is easy to demonstrate that people can and do use their

knowledge of the relative probabilities of English letters in this way, knowledge that often they are not aware they have. For example, one can ask an audience of several hundred people to write down their guess of what the first letter of a preselected six-letter word might be. In an example I demonstrated at a reading conference at York University, the preselected word was *STREAM*. The majority of people will write *E, T, A, I, O, N, S, H, R, D, L,* or *U,* which happen to be the twelve most frequently used English letters in descending order. Scarcely anyone will predict *Z, Y,* or *J*. Usually, *S* happens to be the most common guess for the initial letter of six-letter words, by about one person in eight (as opposed to the one in twenty-six that would be expected if guesses were made at random). Tell an audience that the first letter is indeed *S* and fully half of them will correctly guess the second letter *T* the first time, and fully half again will guess that the third letter is *R*. Most people will then correctly guess that the fourth letter is *E* and go on to be incorrect with their guess that the following letter is another *E,* although they will be correct on their second attempt with *A*. These days, *K* is usually the guess for the final letter, with *M* the successful second guess. In other words, by using their prior knowledge of the relative frequency of letters and groups of letters in English, people rarely have to labor through a dozen or more unsuccessful guesses before they can decide what the next letter of an unknown word might be. The average number of guesses is about three. (The statistically computed average number of alternatives that successive letters of English words might be is seven or eight (Shannon, 1951).

The effect of such prior knowledge is considerable. Most English words remain recognizable if every other letter is obliterated, demonstrating that we scarcely have to look at most letters to identify them in words. A more graphic illustration of the saving that the prior elimination of unlikely alternatives can accomplish is that a single glance at a sequence of random *words* on a screen is usually sufficient to permit the recognition of two or three words, or twice as many letters than could be recognized if the *letters* flashed on the screen had been randomly selected.

But readers know far more about language than the relative likelihood of particular letters in isolated words. We can make excellent guesses about words in sentences. Take any book that happens to be handy, read the last couple of lines of a right-hand page, and then guess what the next word will be when you turn the page. You will not be right every time, of course, but you will almost always guess a word that is possible. Remember, what is important is not to be absolutely correct but to eliminate unlikely alternatives. Once again, statistical analyses of English texts have shown that although in theory authors might draw from a pool of 50,000 words or more for the words to be used in a book, there are on the average no more than 250 alternatives available when they write any particular word in that book (Shannon, 1951). Readers do not need to predict the exact word that will confront them. Nor need they predict more than a few words ahead. But if they can reduce the number of immediate alternatives from many thousands to a couple of hundred, they are taking a considerable burden from the limited information-processing capacity of the brain. Once again our illustrative experiment will demonstrate this saving: if the sequence of thirty letters flashed briefly on a screen comprises a single coherent sentence or meaningful phase, then the viewer can usually see it all at one glance.

There have been hundreds of experiments showing that sequences of letters and words are identified faster, more accurately, and with less visual information, the more they correspond to possible sequences in the English language (a classic example is Tulving and Gold, 1963). The experiments demonstrate not only that individuals, including children, have a considerable prior knowledge of language that enables them to eliminate many unlikely alternatives in advance, but that this knowledge is exercised automatically, without the individual's awareness and without specific instructions to do so. But the prior rejection of unlikely alternatives is a characteristic of the way the human brain works. The reason we are rarely surprised by anything we see, even when we visit an unfamiliar setting, is that we always have a set of prior expectations about what we will in fact see. We do not predict everything; we would be surprised to see a camel in the harbor or a submarine in the zoo, but not vice versa. Nor are our predictions overspecific; we rarely predict *exactly* what we shall see next. Instead, we quite automatically and subconsciously eliminate unlikely possibilities from consideration.

The Advantages of Prediction

Prediction in reading, I have argued, involves the prior reduction of uncertainty by the elimination of unlikely alternatives. We never make our decisions as if we had no prior expectation; recognition and comprehension in such circumstances would always be disruptively time-consuming and tedious. Instead, we seek just enough information to decide among the alternatives that are most likely. As a result, the four limitations on reading that I have discussed as reasons for prediction are very easily overcome, and there are other advantages as well.

Most words have many meanings, but if we are predicting, then we are usually looking for only one meaning of any particular word. You may not be able to guess if the next word is going to be *table* or *chair*, *sideboard*, or *coat-rack*, but if you know that it will refer to a piece of furniture, you will not even consider that *table* might be a set of numbers, or *chair* a verb. The reason speakers and writers are unaware of the potential ambiguity of what they say is that they already know the meaning they are trying to express and do not consider alternative possibilities; they are embarrassed if a double meaning is pointed out to them. Similarly, listeners and readers expect a certain meaning if they are following (or rather predicting) the sense of what they are trying to comprehend; hence puns are so excruciating when eventually we manage to see them. Words may have a multiplicity of meanings and grammatical functions taken one at a time, but in meaningful sentences they are rarely ambiguous.

The pronunciation of words may not be predictable from their spellings, but if you know what a word is likely to be, it is not difficult to use phonics to confirm or reject a particular expectation. As all reading teachers know implicitly, phonics is easy if you already have a good idea what the word is in the first place. Children who can predict that the next word is likely to be either *cow*, *horse*, or *sheep* will not need much knowledge of spelling-to-sound correspondences to decide which it is. In fact it is through such prediction that a mastery of *useful* phonics skills is acquired.

Obviously, prediction will speed up reading and therefore help to overcome the limitation imposed by the brain's rather sluggish rate of information-processing. The fewer alternatives you consider, the faster you can read and the more efficient will be the reading that you accomplish. Reading with prediction means that the brain does not have to waste time analyzing possibilities that could not possibly occur.

The limited capacity of short-term memory is overcome by filling it always with units as large and as meaningful as possible. Instead of being crammed uselessly with half a dozen unrelated letters, short-term memory can contain the same number of words or, better still, the meaning of one or more sentences. In fact, prediction works better at these broader levels; it is easier to predict meanings rather than specific words or letters, and very few letters or words need to be identified to test prediction about meanings.

The first of the bonus advantages of prediction in reading is that the reader is working already at the level of meaning. Reading is meaningful before the reader even begins. Instead of trying to slog through thickets of meaningless letters and words in the fond hope that eventually some nugget of comprehension will arise, the reader is looking for meaning all the time. If any possibility of meaning is to be found in a text, the predicting reader is the one who will find it.

The final advantage is of particular practical importance in many classrooms, namely that with prediction it does not matter if the reader's language does not exactly match that of the writer. All children can understand language that they could not possibly produce; that is why parents quickly learn to conduct their more intimate conversations out of the hearing of their preschool children. Yet the language ability of children in schools is too often evaluated by the speech that they *produce*. Few readers, even adults, can succeed in threshing out the sound of a sentence, word for word, unless they have a good prior idea of what the sentence as a whole means. There is no way children can be expected to identify words as a *preliminary* to getting the meaning if the words are in fact not among those they would choose to express such a meaning. But with prediction, a "one-to-one match" is not required. It will not matter if a child *thinks* the author has written "John ain't got no candy" rather than "John has no candy," provided the meaning is understood and provided the teacher is not demanding literal word-for-word accuracy.

Prediction in the Classroom

Two basic conditions must be met if children are to be able to predict in the manner that is essential for learning to read. The first condition is that the material from which they are expected to learn to read must be potentially meaningful to them; otherwise, there is no way they will be able to predict. The opposite of meaningfulness is nonsense, and anything that is nonsensical is unpredictable. Any material or activity that does not make sense to a child will be more difficult to read.

But meaningfulness of materials and activities is not enough; children must also feel confident that they are at liberty to predict, to make use of what they already know. With prediction there is a constant possibility of error, but then readers who read without ever making errors are not reading efficiently; they are processing far more information than is usually necessary. The child who will become a halting, inefficient reader is one who is afraid to make a mistake. The worst strategy for any reader who is having difficulty understanding text is to slow down and make sure that every word is identified correctly.

The notion that prediction should be encouraged worries many teachers; it may sound as if a virtue is being made out of error. But one should distinguish prediction from reckless guessing. The guesser is usually the child trying to achieve what the teacher is demanding by getting every word right, no matter how little relation it bears to sense. A striking characteristic of older children with low reading ability is that they read as if they have no expectation or interest that the material might make sense but are determined to get the words right at all costs.

Also, accuracy is overrated. There are only two possibilities for a mistake made during reading: either the mistake will make a difference to the meaning, or it will not. If the mistake will make no difference, if the child reads "house" instead of "apartment," then it will make no difference. There is no need to worry. But if the mistake does make a difference, if the child reads "house" instead of "horse," then the reader who is predicting will subsequently notice the anomaly, simply because the meaning is being followed. The child who overlooks obvious errors of sense is not the child who rushes through to understand the gist of a passage but the one who tackles the passage one word at a time.

How, then, can prediction be fostered? There are some obvious techniques, such as encouraging a child to guess what a difficult word might be, and playing reading games in which the teacher stops suddenly, or leaves an occasional word out, or makes an occasional deliberate mistake. But more important, I think, is that prediction should not be discouraged. Prediction is a natural aspect of language. The preferred strategies for children who meet an unfamiliar word in an interesting story are the same as those for fluent readers: first skip, and second, guess. Sooner or later they will have to predict if they are to become fluent readers. Feedback is an essential part of all learning activities, but it can come too soon or too often. A child who pauses before identifying a word may not want the teacher to help "sound it out," nor the rest of the class to tell what it is; the child may in fact know what the word is and simply be wondering what it has to do with the rest of the sentence. A child who "makes a mistake" need not be "corrected" by having the teacher, or the rest of the class, say the right word immediately. If left alone, the child might self-correct in the following sentence, a far more valuable skill in reading than the blind ability to word-call. One of the beautiful advantages of reading *sense* is that it provides its own feedback; errors become self-evident.

One of the most formidable impediments to prediction, at all levels of reading, is anxiety. A child who is afraid to make a mistake is, by definition, anxious, and therefore unwilling to take the necessary risks of prediction. Individuals of any age labelled as reading problems will show anxiety, especially in situations where they feel they are being evaluated; their reluctance to predict will lead to laborious nonsensical reading, and their "difficulty" will become a self-fulfilling prophecy.

Prediction is not everything in reading. Other important considerations include the efficient use of short-term memory, the minimal use of visual cues, and the selection of an appropriate rate of speed for particular reading tasks, together with the acquisition of effective strategies for the identification of unfamiliar words from context. But these are all skills that come primarily through the practice of reading; they are fostered rather than taught (in fact, many teachers are not aware of the extent to which these skills are involved in reading). The advantage of prediction is that it facilitates precisely the kind of confident, successful, and meaningful reading experience through which all of the critical skills of reading are acquired.

4
Learning to Read by Reading

At what point in their literate development can children be said to begin to read? Can the roots of reading be detected before children begin to read in any formal sense?

I have argued elsewhere (Smith, 1971, 1973) that children learn to read by reading, and that a teacher's prime concern must be to do as much reading as is necessary for children until they can make further progress on their own. An occasional objection to this view is that children cannot begin reading until they have mastered some of the mechanics of the task, which usually means some familiarity with phonics. It is also sometimes objected that any "meaningful" approach to reading must surely wait until children can put enough words together to read a meaningful sentence. And a few teachers and theorists have feared that children who have beginning reading made too easy for them might become intellectually lazy and content with minimal progress.

Some insights into all these issues became available recently when I was involved in part of a television film on the topic of reading instruction.[1] As is the nature of both educational research and the filming of young children, the most illuminating incidents occurred when the subject was doing something quite unexpected and even irrelevant to the task at hand. Some events of particular interest also occurred when the camera was not running, so an informal written report may be in order. Since the study involved an N of only one and an observation period of not more than 3 hours, it would be reckless to claim too much generality. Nevertheless, results were obtained which suggest research of a more formal nature and which meanwhile, I think, warrant some thoughtful consideration.

The Case Study

The objectives were clearly defined. I was to take a young child "on the threshold of learning to read" to a supermarket and a department store and demonstrate (1) that the world of children can be full of meaningful print, and (2) that children not only know how to learn, but will always turn to find something to

Reprinted with permission from *Language Arts* 53:297–299, 322, 1976.
[1] *How do you read?* A BBC "Horizon" television film, 1975. Produced by Stephen Rose.

learn if they have exhausted all the learning possibilities of the situation they are in.

The subject was Matthew, aged 3½. He happens to be the older of two children in a middle-class family in suburban Toronto, but there is no reason to suspect that his natural curiosity and learning ability differ markedly from those of other children of about the same age, whatever their sex and family circumstances. Matthew's parents both work, and if anything, he probably watches more television than many children. He is not a precocious reader; his interest in books is limited to looking at their illustrations and having them read to him.

To demonstrate the richness of printed language in Matthew's environment, we first let him wander through the supermarket, following with the camera at eye level. From this perspective it is obvious that Matthew was surrounded by print, reaching literally (but not metaphorically) over his head. There were words all around him, and they were all meaningful, even though most of them were not yet recognizable. He knew that all the words meant something and could certainly distinguish one brand of ketchup from another by the names on the labels. Where did Matthew learn this? Probably from television commercials, which are a rich source of information about reading for children (Torrey, 1970), since commercials frequently present words several times in both their written and spoken form as well as in meaningful contexts.

The amount of written language confronting a child can come as a surprise to an adult who normally pays only passing attention to it. But adult readers have learned to ignore this plethora of print, while to an inquiring, learning child it must be a stimulating situation. It suggests that a child's world may sometimes be as rich in meaningful written language as it is in meaningful spoken language in the home, and it is generally acknowledged that such immersion is essential for learning speech.

There were a few words that Matthew could read on sight and a number that he got wrong, such as "corn flakes" when the package he was looking at gave a brand name. But he knew a good deal about what the print ought to say on a package label, which indicates how well he understood the function of print, and he could apply a probable meaning to a word long before he could recognize the word on sight.

Incidentally, Matthew obviously did not recognize the few words that were familiar to him on the basis of phonics. When asked how he had been able to identify a stop sign correctly, he said it was because it was spelt "*p-o-t-s.*" Does Matthew have a reversal problem? When asked what a street name sign said, he gave the name of his own street, which was nothing like the word he was looking at. Does this mean that Matthew knows nothing about reading, or does it suggest that he will not be long in picking up the additional clues about how to distinguish one word from another, especially since he clearly has a good idea about the alternatives that particular words might be?

In the department store, Matthew was taken to buy a greeting card. Asked if he could identify the sign over the section, he correctly responded "cards." Was he cheating or demonstrating an aspect of reading even though he would not have been able to identify the word out of context? He showed a similar 100-percent ability to predict the sign over the toy department. And he enjoyed this game, although he was not interested in telling us letters. He knew those, so they were boring.

At the luggage department there was a revealing miscue (Goodman, 1969). Matthew took one glance around him and said that the sign said "cases." Would he have done better if he had tried to decode the word by phonics? An answer to that question was suggested when he was tested in the department labelled "footwear." This time the camera was running. Aware, perhaps, that the situation was somehow critical, Matthew now tried to use both a letter-by-letter and a meaning approach. He looked carefully at the sign and its context and said "It either says eff-off or shoes."

To summarize so far, Matthew had made both the points we wanted him to make. A young child can be immersed in printed language, and our sample of one certainly knew how to make sense of it. He also knew how to learn; no one had told him how to use context cues to identify words. Incidentally, it is worth reflecting upon how much a child of Matthew's age can have learned about department stores, not to mention the rest of the world. He was familiar with the layout, knew where he could walk and where not to walk, how items were organized in departments, that they should be paid for, where to pay, how to pay, and to be sure to wait for change. He knew as much as an adult. Who had been giving him all this instruction?

There were still two lessons to be learned by the adults who were following Matthew. Both involved situations in which Matthew might have been said to be acting perversely. He was not doing what we wanted, but his behavior was instructive.

The first occasion was after Matthew had thrown aside in disinterest a book that he had examined with some concentration a few minutes earlier. We thought this action demonstrated that children will not dwell too long in a situation where there is nothing to learn; he had quickly realized that there was nothing further to be gained by studying that book. But when we tried to set up the situation again for filming, Matthew steadfastly refused to reject the book once more. While the camera ground on and on and on, Matthew lay awkwardly immobile on the floor, engrossed in the book, oblivious to any distraction. He had discovered something new, the fact that some pages had a hole in the middle and could be turned by the new method of hooking a finger in them. He was checking to see if every page was the same. He was now demonstrating not that a child will refuse to attend if there is nothing for him to learn, but the complementary point that a child can scarcely be prevented from attending if there is something he wants to learn.

Finally, Matthew picked up a book that he was familiar with, a "scratching book" with pictures of fruit and other objects that gave off an appropriate aroma if their printed surface was scratched with a fingernail. The camera was running and I wanted to turn Matthew's attention elsewhere because I did not want any viewer to conclude from his interest that we might be advocating a smelly-book theory of reading instruction. But Matthew thought I was doubting that the pictures actually smelled so, while the filming continued, he forced me to lower my nose to floor level and sniff at every picture in the book. What did he demonstrate, apart from the well-known propensity of children to embarrass grown-ups in public? He showed that learning for children is an exciting experience which everyone should enjoy. He did not want me to miss the satisfaction of learning something.

Conclusions

At the beginning of this report I stated five issues on which I think my brief case study has had something to say. The first is that children probably begin to read from the moment they become aware of print in any meaningful way, and the second is that the roots of reading are discernable whenever children strive to make sense of print, before they are able to recognize many of the actual words.

Third, not only are the formal mechanics of reading unnecessary in these initial stages, but they may well be a hindrance. It is the ability of children to make sense of the printed word that will enable them to make use of the mechanics we offer. Fourth, words do not need to be in sentences to be meaningful; they just have to be in a meaningful context. It is the reader who brings sense to words. And finally, there is no cause to fear that a child's learning ability will be smothered by too much adult assistance. If children have nothing to learn because they understand the lesson already, they will be bored and will want to move on to something else. But they will also be bored and distractible when there is nothing to learn because they cannot make sense of a task. Therefore, we must be careful to distinguish the two possible causes of inattentiveness.

To sum up, my brief case study tells me that children learn a great deal about reading without adult assistance or even adult awareness. But adults who hope to learn more about learning to read should certainly use the assistance of children.

5
Making Sense of Reading— and of Reading Instruction

Children must have two fundamental insights before they can learn to read. These two insights are rarely discussed in the research literature on reading and are generally ignored in reading instruction, which may even suppress the insights in children who have already managed to acquire them. Without these insights, reading instruction will remain incomprehensible to children and have the adverse effect of making nonsense of reading.

The two fundamental insights are (1) that print is meaningful and (2) that written language is different from speech. I shall discuss each of the two insights in turn, considering first why the insight is essential for learning to read, then how it is normally acquired, and finally how it may be overlooked or even impeded in reading instruction.

Insight 1: Print Is Meaningful

Children are often immersed in spoken language—at home, at play, and even while watching television. But they would make little progress in learning to produce and understand speech unless they could bring meaning to it (Macnamara, 1972), and this would be impossible without the fundamental insight that the sounds of speech are not unrelated to other events but in fact make things happen in the world. Children learn language by making sense of the differences that language makes. By "making sense" I mean that children are able to relate the sounds of the language they hear to understanding they already have. Language makes sense—it is meaningful—when meaning can be brought to it. In fact, I would define *meaning* as "the relevance that can be imposed on an utterance" (Smith, 1975).

It is not clear how or when infants acquire the insight that different sequences of language sounds are related to different meanings, that one sequence of sounds cannot be substituted arbitrarily for another sequence. This insight is unlikely to be explicit; I do not see how adults can explain the meaningfulness of language to children, nor how children might formulate the

Reprinted with permission from *Harvard Educational Review* 47(3): 386–395, 1977.

insight in words for themselves. Rather, I regard the insight as an implicit decision that certain events warrant attention because they are related to situations and intentions that the child can make sense of and is interested in. I suspect that the key lies in Halliday's (1973) observation that children do not learn language independently of its functions. Language, to a child, always has a use, and the various uses could provide the child with a clue to the purposes underlying differences among utterances. A child soon ignores sounds that do not seem to make a difference. There is, in fact, a powerful mechanism in all children preventing them from wasting time on sounds that they cannot make sense of, that do not appear to have a purpose; that mechanism is boredom. Even if the strangeness of the sounds initially stimulates their interest, children will not continue to pay attention to sounds that do not make meaningful differences. That is why they grow up speaking language and not imitating the noise of the air conditioner.

A similar insight—that differences on a printed page have a function, that they are meaningful—must also be the basis for learning written language. As long as children see print as purposeless or nonsensical, they will find attention to print aversive and will be bored. Children will not learn by trying to relate letters to sounds, partly because the task does not make sense to them and partly because written language does not work that way. In my view, reading is not a matter of decoding letters to sound but of bringing meaning to print. Orthography only indirectly relates print to spoken language (Chomsky and Halle, 1968). Phonic generalizations are both cumbersome and unreliable; over 200 rules with hundreds of exceptions apply to the most common words in our language. Relatively few words can be "blended" from the sounds of their spelling. To overcome this problem, instruction usually tries to limit alternatives by placing severe restrictions on the words a child will meet. In normal reading, unlikely alternatives are more efficiently eliminated through the sense of the context. Phonics will never enable a child to decode the words *horse*, *mule*, or *donkey* in isolation. There are at least ten different ways of pronouncing *ho* at the beginning of a word and /horse/ contains one of the uncommon ones; but if context indicates that a word is either *horse*, *mule*, or *donkey*, then phonics will indeed work. My view on this controversial issue is that teachers often give phonics too much credit because of the limited objectives to which phonics are usually directed, and children contribute to the myth because the best readers are always good at phonics. It is, however, the sense of the text, if the text has any sense, that enables readers to use spelling-to-sound correspondences effectively.

Prediction through meaningfulness is the basis of language comprehension. By prediction I do not mean reckless guessing but rather the elimination of unlikely alternatives on the basis of prior knowledge. The child predicts that a limited range of relationships is likely to occur between language and its setting or within the language itself. Meaning, then, is the relationships the child finds. If there is no meaning to be found, there can be no prediction, no comprehension, and no learning. But, to repeat, before meaning can assist a child in learning to read, there must be the insight that print is meaningful.

Acquiring the Insight

Research to date has little to offer in the way of relevant data, but it seems a reasonable hypothesis that the majority of children are as much immersed in written language as in speech. I refer to the wealth of print to be found on every product in the bathroom, on every jar and package in the kitchen, in the television guide and television commercials, in comics, catalogs, advertising fliers, street signs, store fronts, billboards, supermarkets, and department stores. All of this print is meaningful; it makes a difference. We do not expect corn flakes in a package labelled "detergent."

The question is whether children who cannot yet read pay very much attention to all this print. I have reported on a 3½-year-old boy who obviously could not read the words *luggage* and *footwear* on signs in a department store but who nevertheless asserted that the first sign said "cases" and the second said "shoes." Here was one child who could bring meaning to print long before he could read the actual words, who had acquired the insight that differences in print are meaningful.

I can think of only one way in which such an insight might be achieved and that is when a child is being read to or observes print being responded to. At this point, I am not referring to the reading of books or stories but to the occasions when a child hears "That sign says 'stop'," "That word is 'boy'," or "There's the bus for downtown." Television commercials may do the same for a child. They not only announce in spoken and written language the product's name, desirability, and uniqueness, but they also demonstrate the product at work. The point in all of these cases is that no substitution could be made; the print is directly related to the setting in which it occurs, just as is the spoken language of the home. Once the fundamental insight about the meaningfulness of written language is attained, I see no reason why children should not go on spontaneously elaborating upon it as they do with speech. Children can test hypotheses about the meaning of the printed word *toys* not because anyone reads it to them but because it indicates the location of the toy department.

The Relevance of Instruction

I must reiterate that to make sense of any aspect of language a child must perceive a purpose for it. In school, I believe, this need implies that children must understand not only the content of the instruction—the materials they are expected to read—but also the purpose of the instruction. However, this often does not occur, and in the next few paragraphs I describe what I consider to be some aspects of reading instruction which are fundamentally incomprehensible.

One such aspect is the decomposition of spoken words to sounds. The spoken word *cat* makes sense in some contexts, but the sounds /kuh/, /a/, /tuh/ do not. It should not be surprising that children find it difficult to detect these units in speech (until and unless they catch on to the highly conventionalized game that is being taught), because such units do not, in fact, exist in spoken language, where individual sounds and even words are slurred together. Speech is certainly not understood through an analysis and subsequent synthesis of its parts (Liberman, 1970). Auditory acuity is not essential for reading, although it may be a prerequisite for reading instruction.

Another incomprehensible exercise is the decomposition of written words to letters. The printed word *cat* can make sense in some contexts, since it refers to an object in the real world with which children can meaningfully interact. But the letters *c*, *a*, and *t* do not have that status. They refer to specialized visual symbols that have nothing to do with anything else in the child's life. Until children have had substantial experience reading, they must find it profoundly unsettling to be confronted with the information that *cat* begins with /see/ or that *bat* and *ball* both start with the same letter. Children who know the alphabet tend to be good readers, but teaching letter names will not turn a poor reader into a good one (Samuels, 1972). Rather, it would seem, fluency with the alphabet comes with being a competent reader.

A third problematic aspect of instruction is the relating of letters to sounds. For a child who has no conception of reading to be told that some peculiar shapes called "letters" (which have no apparent relevance in the real world) are related in any way to some improbable sounds (which have no existence in the real world) must be the purest jabberwocky. Of course, with a certain amount of goodwill and diligence a child might succeed in learning to recite a few of these correspondences. At best, however, such correspondences will not make sense until the child is able to read; at worst, they may persuade the child that reading is a matter of trying to produce meaningless sounds at an impossibly high speed.

The use of metalinguistic terms poses yet other problems. Many of the words that children are expected to understand in order to benefit from reading instruction, in fact, make sense only when one is able to read. The word *letter* is a case in point and so is the word *word*. The status of a word in spoken language is extremely dubious; words cannot be segregated by any mechanical or electronic device from the continuous flow of normal speech (Cherry, 1966), and linguists prefer not to use the term at all. The usual definitions of a *word*—"letters surrounded by white space" or "a separate item in a dictionary"—obviously apply only to written language. It should not be surprising that many novice readers cannot make sense of this and other metalinguistic terms, such as *sentence, paragraph, capital letter*, or even *space*, since only more skilled readers have experienced them meaningfully. Teaching children the definitions of such terms will not make them readers (Downing and Oliver, 1974), because until they can read, the terms will remain entirely senseless to them.

Finally, many drills and exercises are meaningless. It does not matter how much a teacher might believe or hope that certain exercises have a point; anything that is opaque to a child can contribute nothing positive to reading. Children frequently learn to achieve high scores on boring, repetitive, and nonsensical tasks (especially, once more, those children who happen to be competent readers), but such a specialized skill will not make children into readers. Low scores, on the other hand, can certainly interfere with reading development and not simply because children risk being stigmatized as potential poor readers, but because they may begin to regard rote, meaningless, and difficult activities as a model for how reading is employed.

The content of the material which children are expected to begin reading may also be incomprehensible. As a general rule, isolated words, which are the basis of much initial reading instruction, make no more sense than isolated letters. However, words in a meaningful context—if a child is encouraged to use context—promote prediction, comprehension, and learning. But some elaboration is required. Words that appear by themselves are not necessarily meaningless. In the world outside school, individual words—for example, *gas, exit, burgers*—make a lot of sense. But these single words are not, in fact, devoid of context; they are given meaning and function by the settings in which they are found. This is not the case when individual words are isolated from any apparent function and are printed alone in lists, on chalkboards, in exercise books, and even under some pictures. Many of the words that are likely to appear in isolation in school have a multiplicity of meanings and grammatical functions. Words like *shoe, house,* and *chalk* can be nouns or verbs, and *open* and *empty* can be adjectives or verbs. To ask children to identify such words is simply to ask them to put a name to them, not a meaning. Conversely, the fact that a word is embedded in a grammatical sentence does not make it meaningful. Sentences can be just as devoid of purpose and meaning as isolated words (*Sam the fat cat sat on the flat mat*) and so can whole paragraphs and "stories" made up of such sentences.

A consequence of all this potential meaninglessness in reading instruction may be to confound children who are striving to learn through making sense of what they are doing. More seriously, the ultimate danger is that children who do not have the insight that written language should make sense will never achieve it, while children who have got it may be persuaded that they are wrong. Unfortunately, a good deal of reading instruction seems to be based on the premise that sense should be the last, not the first, concern of readers.

Such instruction may not be ineffectual. Many students identified as having reading problems in high school struggle to get every word right, drawing on all their resources of phonics, and in this way they may succeed. But they show no apparent concern for meaning and no evident expectation that sense has any bearing on what they are trying to do. As a cure for their obvious disability, they may often be removed entirely from any possibility of reading meaningful text and returned to a meaningless form of beginning reading. Such meaningless materials and activities are occasionally supposed to exemplify "getting back to basics."

Insight 2: Print Is Different From Speech

Obviously, spoken language and written language are not the same. It is not difficult to detect when a speaker is reading from a prepared text, especially one written for publication, or when a speaker is reading the unedited transcript of a spontaneous talk. Speech and print are not different languages; they share a common vocabulary and the same grammatical forms. But they are likely to contain different distributions of each. It is not surprising that differences exist between spoken and written language, since each is frequently used for quite different purposes and audiences. Spoken language itself varies radically, depending on the purpose for which it is used and the relationships among the people using it. Although it is difficult to specify exactly how or why written and spoken language differ, I believe this difference has a simple and distinct basis: spoken language has adapted itself to being heard while written language is more appropriately read.

To understand how such specialized adaptation might have come about, it is necessary to examine the different demands that the two language forms make upon their recipients. For example, consider the obvious fact that spoken language is ephemeral. The word dies the moment it is uttered and can be recaptured only if it is held in one's fallible memory or if one asks the speaker to go to the trouble of recapitulating. In contrast to the facile way in which we can move back and forth through written text, even tape recording does little to mitigate the essential transience of speech. Writing, unlike speech, is largely independent of the constraints of time. Put in another way—and this is still an untested hypothesis—spoken language often makes a considerable short-term demand on memory while written language does not. The reader can not only attend to several words at a time but can also select what those words will be, the order in which they will be dealt with, and the amount of time that will be spent on them.

There is, however, another demand that written language places upon the reader, related not to memory but to the far more fundamental question of how we make sense of language in the first place. The question concerns how language is verified—how we confirm that the information we are receiving is true, that it makes sense, or, indeed, that we understand the message correctly. For everyday spoken language, the matter of verification is simple: Look around. An utterance is usually related to the situation in which it occurs. But if we do not understand or believe what we read, the ultimate recourse can only be back to the text itself. With written language, difficult and possibly unique skills are required in order to verify, disambiguate, and avoid error. Specifically, the skills involve following an argument, looking for internal consistencies, and thinking abstractly.

These requirements of written language have so impressed some theorists that they have argued that writing has introduced a whole new mode to our repertoire of intellectual skills (Havelock, 1976; Goody and Watt, 1968; Olson, 1977). It might be objected that spoken language is often as abstract, argumentative, and unrelated to the circumstances in which it is comprehended as a scientific paper. But Olson (1977) claims that our ability to produce and understand such spoken language is simply a by-product of our being literate. Only because of our experience in reading can we make sense of abstract speech, which in its form is more like writing than everyday spoken language.

The Need for the Insight

Children who expect to read in the way they make sense of spoken language are likely to have difficulty in comprehending print and thus in learning to read. Their predictions will be all wrong. It does not matter that we cannot define exactly the differences between spoken and written language. We cannot say what the rules of spoken language are; yet children learn to make sense of speech. Nor is there convincing evidence that children need to have the conventions of written language explained to them, provided they can make sense of print. The general requirements of immersion in the problem, of making sense, and of getting feedback to test hypotheses would seem to be just as easily met with written language as with speech. In fact, since a number of alternative tests can be conducted on the same material, written language might seem to have advantages as far as hypothesis-testing is concerned. By virtue of its internal consistency, the text itself can provide feedback about the correctness of hypotheses, just as the surrounding situation may provide feedback that is relevant to speech. When reading something you comprehend, you can usually tell if you make a mistake that makes a difference—for the very reason that it *makes* a difference—and you can probably go back to find out why. However, none of this will be of any value to children learning to read if the language from which they are expected to learn is not in fact written language or if they do not have the fundamental insight that written language and speech are not the same.

Acquiring the Insight

How might children acquire and develop the insight that speech and written language are not the same? There can be only one answer: by hearing written language read aloud. When a child's predictions about written language fail because they are based on prior knowledge of spoken language, then an occasion exists for gaining the insight that spoken and written language are different. As written language is heard and comprehended, hypo-thesis-testing will also help children develop an implicit under-standing of the particular characteristics of written language. And children can considerably augment this understanding as they become able to do more and more of their own reading.

I suspect it is the higher probability of hearing written lan-guage that accounts for the finding that children tend to become proficient readers if they come from homes where a good deal of reading occurs. (Sartre [1964] has related his experience of learn-ing to read in this way.) Children are unlikely to learn to read by osmosis (by the mere fact that books are around them), from direct parental instruction, or because they see the value of read-ing by watching adults perform what initially must seem a pretty meaningless, silent activity. Rather, I would be inclined to credit the simple possibility that such children are more likely than other children to hear written language being read.

Actual stories are the kind of reading that I think most familiar-izes children with written language. These can range from the contemporary material found in newspapers and magazines, elaborating perhaps upon something already experienced, to the traditional content of fairy tales and adventure stories, to history and myth. These traditional stories fascinate children—possibly fulfilling some of their deepest needs (Bettelheim, 1976)—without pandering to an alleged inability to handle complex language or ideas. All of these story types are truly written language, pro-duced for a purpose in a conventional medium. There is no evidence that children find it harder to understand such complex texts (when they are read to them) than to understand complex adult speech. In both cases it usually does not matter if large parts of the language are incomprehensible, provided the general theme and interest carry the reader or listener along. Indeed, it is through exposure to such meaningful complexity that children are able to develop and test their hypotheses about the nature of spoken or written language.

Most of the material that interests children at school—and from which they would be likely to learn—tends to be too difficult for them to read by themselves. This poses a problem for teach-ers. One solution would be to help children read or listen to such material. But the alternative often selected is to seek or produce less complex material—pseudoforms—in the expectation that children will find them simpler. And if this specially tailored material also confounds beginners, the assumption may be made that the fault lies with the children or with their language de-velopment.

Indeed, the language of school texts is probably unfamiliar to most children. But this situation need not have its roots in the particular kind of spoken language with which a child is familiar nor even in the child's possibly limited experience with print. The source is more likely to be the artificial language of school books, whether of the truncated "cat on the mat" variety or the more florid "Down the hill hand in hand skipped Susie and her friend." This language is so different from any other spoken or written form that it is probably most appropriate to put it into an exclusive category, "school language."

Of course, such language tends to be quite unpredictable for many children, who may then have enormous difficulty understanding and learning to read from it. Ironically, it is often concluded that written language is intrinsically difficult for children who would be better off learning from "spoken language written down." The source for such a hybrid is either someone's intuition of what constitutes spoken language or, worse still, a dialect of that language, or even "children's language," the description of any of which confounds professional linguists. The result may be something that is quite unlike written language yet has none of the advantages of everyday speech, since it has to be comprehended out of its setting. Children may learn to recite such print, but I have seen no evidence that it makes them readers. And any insight they might have in advance about the nature of written language is likely to be undermined. Worse, children may be persuaded that the print they first experience in school is a model for all the written language that will confront them throughout their lives, a conviction that would be as discouraging as it is misleading.

Conclusions

I have argued that children need two basic insights to begin to learn to read. Also, I have implied that with these insights children can solve by themselves all the other problems associated with print, provided that no extraneous confusion or hindrance is put in their way. They must be able to predict and make sense of language in the first place, and they can do this only by bringing meaning to it. This is certainly the way that all children learn spoken language and is probably the reason that many of them succeed in learning to read despite the instructional method used.

As I have argued elsewhere, the implications for instruction are that a child learns to read by reading and that the teacher's role is to make reading easy. I do not mean that reading is made easy by the use of simple material, which can indeed be difficult because of its probable irrelevance and unpredictability. Rather, I suggest helping children to understand any written material that interests them—whether the help is provided by the teacher, an aide, another child, or a tape recording—or simply by permitting children to make errors and omissions without penalty and without the disruption of unwanted correction. Children seek help when they need it and ignore it when they do not.

There are, of course, many factors that can contribute to failure in reading, including lack of motivation, low expectations, fear of failure, and hostility to the school or to the teacher. But failure also implies that a child sees no sense in what is involved in learning to read. A child's commitment to learn reflects an economic decision made on the basis of perceived cost and return. The problem for the teacher is not just to make reading comprehensible (which may be hard enough) but also to make sure that the instruction makes sense and is relevant to all of the child's concerns. Children who can make sense of instruction should learn to read; children confronted by nonsense are bound to fail. The issue is as simple—and as complicated—as that.

6
The Uses of Language

What is the use of language? The question is not an idle one, because no one—except possibly linguists in their more recondite moments—is interested in language independent of its utility or consequences. Certainly children do not learn language as an abstract system but as something they can use and understand in their interactions with the world around them. I propose that the uses to which language is put lie at the heart of language comprehension and learning, and that the uses of language must therefore be a constant concern for language teachers.

Halliday (1973) points out that children do not learn language which they *then* apply to various functions; they learn language *as* they learn its functions. This observation has a number of practical implications—that language is unlikely to be learned in situations where it has no apparent utility, that mastery of some uses for language does not entail familiarity with all its uses, and conversely, that inability to employ language for some purposes does not necessitate a lack of competence in language itself.

My direction in this paper will be to explore the intentions of language users, and I shall do this by listing some of the uses to which language is put. I shall be looking at language not as a system, which is what the linguist does, but as a tool, which I think is how it is perceived by children. My perspective will be that comprehension of language on any occasion is clearly related to comprehension of the use to which it is put. And I shall try to show that language is a tool that has many uses. There is no simple answer to my opening question about the use of language, because language manifests itself across the entire range of human interests and intentions. To say that language is used "for communication" or "to convey information" is to beg the question, because these terms themselves demand elucidation. A paper not much different from the present one would be required to expand upon "the uses of communication."

My object is to reflect upon the scope of language and to demonstrate that there is nothing that is unique about the uses that it serves. There are always other ways of trying to achieve the ends for which language is employed. An important theoretical and practical implication of the preceding statement is that language uses are themselves not developed in a vacuum, but rather

Reprinted with permission from *Language Arts* 54(6):638–644, 1977.

are overlaid on other means of achieving the same ends. Language learning literally depends on the user's intentions. To understand language and to teach it we must understand the mind of the language learner.

Elsewhere I have argued that there is nothing about language *learning* that is unique (Smith, 1975). The innate learning ability that enables infants to solve fundamental problems about the nature of the world in general is sufficient to enable a child to discover the rules and uses of speech, and subsequently to learn to read. The argument can even be extended to second-language learning (Fillion, Smith, and Swain, 1976). Now I want to show that language has no uses for which other means are not available, that there is nothing about language *use* that is unique. In fact (and this was a surprise to me when I first contemplated the uses of language), language may be the universal all-purpose tool. It can be recruited to assist in every enterprise that motivates human beings. Language may extend the possibilities of the human mind, but it does not create new ones. Language and human intentions are inseparable.

A List of Language Uses

My list is intended simply to illustrate the range of uses to which language can be put. The list can by no means be considered to be complete; indeed, such a catalog would have to cover all of human psychology. Nor can the list claim to be a taxonomy, since it is not ordered in any particular way nor is there any indication of how the different categories might be related to each other. It is not even a very good list, since the categories are certainly not exhaustive and are probably overlapping. And finally, the list is hardly original, since I have taken the first seven headings directly from Halliday (1973) and have added only three of my own.

I have turned to Halliday because he has, with his "seven models of language," gone into rather more detail about the actual circumstances of language use than the many theorists— starting with Plato and including Halliday himself—who have tried to compress language even further into a few basic "functions," usually related to its expressive, communicative, and descriptive aspects. But these aspects I see more as general descriptions of language than as summaries of its uses.

I shall, in fact, avoid the usual term *functions* since it seems to me to detract from the extreme flexibility with which language is employed. Functions reside in objects—according to one dictionary definition, they are "the reason a thing exists"—while uses are determined by users. It is not a function of forks to comb the hair, but they may be used for that purpose. Knives are designed for specialized functions of cutting but can be used for a variety of ends, from digging holes to opening locked doors, bounded only by the imagination of the user. Perhaps language should not be said to have functions at all in the sense of having been designed or developed for specific purposes; rather, it has persisted and developed over time for the simple reason that it adapts to so many useful ends.

The following list is divided into two parts. On the left are ten general uses to which language may be put, indicated by a broadly descriptive label and followed by a brief example and explanatory elaboration. Halliday was also the source for the first seven of the phrases that epitomize the particular language use, e.g., "I want" for the instrumental use of language. On the right of the list I have added for each item an alternative nonlanguage means by which the particular use to which language is put might also be accomplished.

Language use	*Nonlanguage alternative*
Instrumental: "I want." (Language as a means of getting things, satisfying material needs.)	Pantomime, facial expressions, screaming, pointing, grabbing.
Regulatory: "Do as I tell you." (Controlling the behavior, feelings, or attitudes of others.)	Pushing and pulling people around; modelling behavior for others to copy.
Interactional: "Me and you." (Getting along with others, establishing relative status. Also, "Me against you"— establishing separateness.)	Waving, smiling, linking arms, holding hands, shaking fists; sport.
Personal: "Here I come." (Expressing individuality, awareness of self, pride.)	Art, music, dress, cosmetics, ornamentation.
Heuristic: "Tell me why?" (Seeking and testing knowledge.)	Exploration, investigation, experimentation.

(continued)

Language use	Nonlanguage alternative
Imaginative: "Let's pretend." (Creating new worlds, making up stories, poems.)	Play, art, mime.
Representational: "I've got something to tell you." (Communicating information, descriptions, expressing propositions.)	Pointing, rituals, diagrams, maps, mathematics.
Diversionary: "Enjoy this." (Puns, jokes, riddles.)	Games, puzzles, magic.
Authoritative/contractual: "How it must be." (Statutes, laws, regulations, agreements, contracts.)	Roles, rituals, regalia, uniforms, architecture.
Perpetuating: "How it was." (Records, histories, diaries, notes, scores.)	Photographs, sculpture, monuments, memorials.

Observations

I have no simple moral or conclusion to offer from the preceding list. Instead I have a dozen observations to make, all of them tentative but all, I think, relevant both to the study of language and to the practices of language instruction. The observations are listed in the form of assertions, but I regard them basically as questions requiring further reflection and research, especially with respect to their implications for education. Some at least might strike a responsive note in different readers. The first few observations are concerned primarily with the construction of the list, the later ones more with its implications. But there is no point at which a dividing line might be drawn.

First. Even a tenfold categorization oversimplifies all the varied uses of language. The "perpetuating" use, for example, could easily be divided into *mnemonic* (diary notes, a knot in a handkerchief) and *memorial* (a testament, the Taj Mahal). A good deal of semantic juggling would be required to fit some examples of language under one or even a combination of the ten categories. Lying, for example, does not seem to me to find a natural place, nor do sermons, prayers, graffiti, bumper stickers, language used to cover embarrassment, the pointless language of many beginning readers and workbooks, and writing produced simply for the joy of producing writing (a pleasure often marked in children).

Second. Language generates a number of uses related only to itself. (Language used to talk about language is known as *metalanguage*.) Much of school language is metalanguage, whether the topic is sounds, letters, phonics, parts of speech, sentences, punctuation, grammar, definitions, "concepts," logic, rhetoric, "reasoning," or philosophy. All of this immense (and, to a child, largely unfamiliar) superstructure of language may have little practical use outside the system itself.

Third. The point seems self-evident but is, I think, enormously important, especially in education, that skill in one use of language need not generalize to skill in others. Even articulate adults can be relatively awkward in exercising or appreciating some uses of language—for example, the interactional or the diversionary—especially if they are not entirely familiar with the particular language or the culture in which it is spoken. Children newly arrived at school may find little of the supportive interactional language to which they are highly tuned and a good deal of representational language which is largely foreign to them.

Fourth. Language is not usually employed for just one use at a time. Halliday (1973) distinguished most of his seven functions of language in the first few months of a child's linguistic life and says they become merged into a smaller number of "macrofunctions" and "megafunctions" with the development of grammar. Certainly, speech that is "impersonal," without an interactional component, is not usually regarded by children as neutral but rather as negatively interactional, i.e., rejecting. Children may not expect an adult to use "detached" language without good reason.

Fifth. Different language modalities do not serve the various uses equally well. Writing, for example, is probably more efficient than speech with respect to permanency and also for authority and commitment (contracts are usually in writing). On the other hand, speech is often better for many interactional and personal uses.

Sixth. Language is not necessarily more efficient in some of its uses than the nonlanguage alternatives that are available. Language is not conspicuously effective in expressing emotion or deep feelings (compared, for example, with dancing) and may be less adequate than a touch of the hand to convey affection or condolence. Language can fail in its instrumental or regulatory uses, in which case there appears to be a natural temptation to "regress" to earlier means of expressing determination, frustration, and outrage. Language by itself is not particularly efficient in teaching skills such as swimming, bicycle riding, or reading, although it may be useful for describing or highlighting particular points of instruction (Olson and Bruner, 1974).

Seventh. As listed, each of the language uses involves at least one other person, a listener or reader, apart from the actual language user. But each use of language and each of the non-language alternatives can be conducted—or at least rehearsed—wholly within the mind of the individual. The imagination can be an arena for developing and practising all the uses of language and their alternative means.

Eighth. The list is also incomplete because it considers language primarily from the point of view of the intentions of its producers, speakers, or writers. But listeners and readers have intentions also, although the use they make of an instance of language may not be identical or even complementary to the purpose of its producer. As a demonstration, one of my seminar groups recently listed down the center of several sheets of paper a large number of different examples of printed language—novels, poetry, menus, street signs, telephone directories, television guides, instruction manuals, diaries, and so forth. On the left of this list they noted the probable intention or motivation of the producer of each particular piece of writing and on the right side the probable intention or motivation of a reader. They found little correspondence between the two sides of the list. Similarly with spoken language, particular utterances seemed likely to have different meanings to the speaker and the listener. This observation might seem to support my earlier contention that comprehension is always relative to the particular purposes or intentions of the comprehender. It also illustrates the futility of trying to provide simple answers to overgeneral questions like "What is reading?" or "What is comprehension?".

Ninth. The preceding observation suggests both a cause and possible way out of the perennial dilemma about the nature of meaning. Normally when we say "What do you mean?" to someone we do not understand, we are probably asking something like "What is your intention in saying or writing that; what end are you trying to achieve?" And while it is a useful shortcut to ask "What does that sentence (or utterance) mean?" it should be recognized that the question really is "What was the intention or purpose behind that sentence?" But the ostensibly innocuous change of word order from "What does that sentence mean?" to "What is the meaning of that sentence?" can lead to the impression that the meaning, or some kind of purpose or intention, resides in the sentence itself, and from there to the difficult question "What is meaning?" As long as meaning is not detached from the producer's purpose or intention, there is little chance of semantic or philosophical confusion. The term is similarly clear and comprehensible as long as it is related to a listener's or reader's interpretation and intentions.

This close relationship of meaning and intention is particularly apparent in the way the word *mean* occurs in such common usages as "What do you mean, 'Pass the jam'?" when we understand very well that the person wants the jam—the instrumental use. Rather we are commenting on the interactional use of language, as we show when we add "Don't you mean 'Pass the jam *please*'?"

Tenth. This is one of my major points: for every use of language distinguished in the previous list there is a nonlanguage alternative. The interesting theoretical question that arises is whether each language use is in fact *based on* the related nonlanguage alternative? In other words, will the language use fail to develop until the individual has the nonlanguage alternative means to build it on? Such a possibility would imply that language adds nothing new to the repertoire of human skills—the potential for every use of language must exist prior to the use of language itself.

Eleventh. Implications follow for language instruction. If every use of language depends upon a prior nonlanguage alternative, then the most effective way to develop language use, and thereby language fluency, would be through the underlying nonlanguage means. Indeed, until a child can achieve a particular end without language, there will be little point in expecting language to be used in a particular way. The way to promote in children the difficult representational or descriptive function of language, for example, might lie in the simultaneous or even prior encouragement of alternative forms of representation, such as drawing, model building, or play generally.

Finally. Is there anything left? By this I mean is there any human intention for which language cannot be recruited? A negative answer would, I think, put a new light on the relationship between human beings and their language; it would show that language defines the limits of human possibility. While language may only be a reflection of what makes us human, it reflects *everything* that makes us human.

Perhaps it is not language at all that makes human beings different from other animals, but the uses to which language is put, the ends that we can also accomplish in other ways but which other animals cannot perhaps accomplish at all. Human beings engage in a number of activities that distinguish them from other animals—mathematics, music, rituals, art, ornamentation, sport (all items, you will notice, on the nonlanguage side of my list). Even if we think we can observe suggestions of such behaviors in lower animals, the behaviors are instinctive and inevitable, exercised without either flexibility or self-consciousness. Birds may sing, but they don't go to concerts. The difference may lie in the self-regarding intentions of humankind. Sometimes it is argued that language generates self-awareness, but perhaps there could be no language without it.

If it is the case that mastery of language uses depends on familiarity with alternative means of achieving the same ends, then indeed the only way to promote language skills in children would be to foster their more general development, especially their self-awareness, and to extend their interactions with others and with the world. On the other hand, interference with their language in any way would interfere with the development of the children themselves. Where children exhibit reluctance or apprehension about any aspect of language learning or use, one should perhaps look for a failure of education, an inhibition rather than an inability.

Conclusion

The only firm conclusion I want to draw at this stage is a further observation: that a good deal more thought should be given to the ways in which language is used, in school and out, and to the ways in which we expect language and its uses to be learned.

7
Conflicting Approaches to Reading Research and Instruction

My theme is that there are two quite distinct ways of conceptualizing reading but that one of these perspectives tends to predominate when reading is considered from an experimental point of view. As a result, there is a critical bias in reading theory and research that has been extended to a bias in classroom practice, a bias that limits and possibly distorts the way many people think about reading and reading instruction. The greater part of this chapter is concerned with the cause, nature, and consequences of this bias, first in reading theory and then when theory is "translated" into practice. However, I conclude with a few general cautions about the application of theory to practice and some remarks about other issues that have tended to be of lesser concern in reading research but that may, in fact, be of major relevance to reading instruction.

Opposing Theoretical Approaches to Reading

Although there are numerous theories of reading, they can, in general, be grouped into two distinct categories, depending on where the source and control of any particular reading act is presumed to lie. Many theories view reading as a process that begins with the print on the page and ends with some representation or interpretation inside the brain. I call such theories "outside-in theories." The other class of theories perceives reading as a highly discriminative process that begins in the brain and ends with selective attention to only part of the printed text. I call such theories "inside-out theories."

Outside-in theories are clearly dominant in both the research literature and instructional development. They are characterized by the notion that everything on a page of text is "processed" and that reading is primarily a hierarchical series of decisions—first letters are discriminated, then they are synthesized into words (usually, but not always, through "decoding" into a phonological or "underlying" level of spoken language), as a consequence of which comprehension takes place. It would be invidious to identi-

Reprinted with permission from Lauren B. Resnick and Phyllis A. Weaver (Eds.), *Theory and Practice of Early Reading* (Vol. 2). Hillsdale, N.J.: Erlbaum, 1979.

fy one or two of these theories, and I have neither the space nor the inclination to list them all. Examples proliferate in such compilations as Kavanagh and Mattingly (1972) and the final report of the U.S. Office of Education Targeted Research and Development Program in Reading (Davis, 1971). They also account for a large proportion of the studies reported in *Reading Research Quarterly* and predominate in most psychological and linguistic speculation about reading. Outside-in theories are frequently detectable from a distance by virtue of their elaborate flowcharts, with arrows leading from the "stimulus" of print through iconic storages, scanners, comparators, and decoders to destination boxes labelled "semantic store" or, quite simply, "meaning."

There is, in fact, no evidence that any reader pays attention to every letter—or in many circumstances, to every word—in any natural reading situation. Neither eye-movement studies nor analyses of oral reading indicate just how much or how little of the actual print readers "process" when they are reading meaningful text, although it is obvious that readers often identify words without attending to all the letters on the page, and that they can also make sense of text without identifying all the particular words in front of their eyes. Almost all the experimental work that has provided the conceptual basis for outside-in theories of reading has been done with tachistoscopic equipment and meaningless materials in unmotivated laboratory situations.

My main criticism of outside-in theories is not so much that they are wrong as that they are not representative. They provide reliable and replicable data about how individuals respond when confronted with atypical "identification" tasks in laboratory settings, but in fact they bear little resemblance to what takes place when individuals normally read street signs, telephone directories, labels, menus, newspaper reports, poetry, or anything else that is interesting or informative to them. More specifically, outside-in theories fail to account for *intention* (we usually read for a purpose), *selectivity* (we attend only to what we want and need to know), *prediction* (we are rarely bewildered or surprised by anything that we read), and *comprehension* (we are rarely aware of the enormous potential ambiguity, both syntactic and semantic, of the most common words and constructions of our language). It is invariably easier to read meaningful texts than nonsensical strings of words, just as letters in words are easier to identify than letters occurring randomly. In fact, we are normally aware of words only when meaning fails, and we attend to letters only when words are unfamiliar—the reverse of the outside-in view. Of course, the fact that readers are usually aware only of meaning does not logically entail that they are giving no attention to letters and words in the process, but the absence of direct or introspective evidence is hardly support for the outside-in point of view.

The selectivity that characterizes meaningful reading is not something that outside-in theories can cope with simply by appeal to specialized "filters" or by the introduction of additional arrows pointing upstream in the flowcharts and labelled "feedback" or "prediction." Nor can such theories assert that the reader looks for and processes "higher order invariances" or "largest meaningful units" without acknowledging that what determines the size of a unit is not the nature of the print on the page but the intention of the reader in the first place, an inside-out perspective.

The inside-out view begins with intention: It regards reading as a truly active, centrally motivated and centrally directed process in which readers hypothesize, or predict, among a certain range of meaningful likely alternatives and search and analyze among the featural information available in the print only to the extent necessary to resolve their remaining uncertainty. The inside-out view endeavors to account for the identification of words without the mediation of letter identification (readers search for features to decide among alternative word possibilities independently of a feature search to identify letters). It tries to explain why letters in words are easier to identify than letters in random sequences and why words in meaningful sequences are easier to identify than random words. In each case, a set of expectancies is established on the basis of prior knowledge, reducing the number of alternatives considered by readers. Readers look for the featural information that they need and ignore information that is irrelevant or redundant to their purposes. The inside-out perspective does not require recourse to spoken language for the comprehension of print. Meaning is directly accessible through print (as exemplified in the visible difference in meaning between *their* and *there*) and, in fact, it must be determined before the text can be read aloud in a comprehensible manner. Without prior comprehension, many words cannot even be allocated a grammatical function (for example, is *house* a noun or a verb?), let alone an appropriate pronunciation or intonation.

Inside-out theories are by no means adequate, of course. Indeed, when one considers the enormity of the attempt to understand how knowledge of the world is organized and integrated in the human brain, which is the beginning of the inside-out analysis of reading, then one comprehends why it has been asserted more than once that to understand reading would be the acme of a psychologist's achievement (Huey, 1908/1968; Neisser, 1967). But the acme of a psychologist's achievement is surely not a series of reaction-time studies measuring how long it takes individuals to name letters and words. Gough (1972) acknowledged the root of the problem when he characterized the end point of his outside-in theory of reading as "the place where sentences go when they are understood," reached by a procedure that he left in the hands of a wizard in the head named Merlin. Such a magical approach cannot explain why readers remain unaware of letters or even words in the process of understanding sentences, nor why they are also unaware of potential ambiguities and even of the meaningful mistakes that all readers make from time to time. Normal reading seems to begin, proceed, and end in meaning, and the source of meaningfulness must be the prior knowledge in the reader's head. Nothing is comprehended if it does not reflect or elaborate on what the reader already knows.

It can rightly be objected that inside-out theories are vague. However, not enough is known about the way individual human knowledge is organized to provide a basis for more than cautious speculation. On the other hand, outside-in theories do not get very far in. Can "reading" really be studied if it stops short of comprehension?

Apart from the conceptual conundrums confronted by inside-out theories, they are also handicapped by the difficulty of designing "critical" experiments. Because of their scope and the inherent problem of exercising laboratory control in situations in which the major variable is something as unpredictable as an individual's prior knowledge and intentions, very few experimental paradigms for studying comprehension lend themselves to simple replication or quantitative analysis. Even the most compelling studies of language comprehension can be regarded only as illustrative. Most of the data relevant to inside-out theories of reading and language comprehension are based on anecdote, observation, or introspection, but so too are many of the studies on which today's powerful theories of spoken language acquisition are based.

Conversely, I think the dominance of outside-in theories in the research literature is entirely attributable to their conceptual simplicity and experimental tractability. It is far easier to design replicable experiments, conduct statistical analyses, and achieve reliable results when the concern is limited to reaction times to meaningless letters and words. When subjects succeed in imposing meaning on such tasks—by relating the stimuli to something they know beyond the constraints of the task—the well-ordered predictability of results breaks down. Meaning makes such tasks easier for subjects but harder for experimenters; thus, most outside-in studies of reading require that the subject be the most unrepresentative of all readers—an individual with no relevant prior knowledge or expectations about the task at hand.

Such essential nonsense in outside-in reading research mirrors the 100-year study of nonsense in experimental psychology's investigation of "verbal learning." Since the invention of the nonsense syllable, this investigation has been a constant battle between subjects striving to make sense of their tasks and experimenters trying to devise more effective nonsense, because it is only with nonsense that psychology's venerable "laws of learning" apply (Smith, 1975, Chapter 5).

Preoccupation with the alphabetic nature of the particular written language with which they are usually concerned is a marked characteristic of outside-in theories. Reading is frequently seen as simply a matter of "decoding" these alphabetic symbols into sound by the application of spelling-to-sound correspondence rules, although the theoretical or empirical necessity for such decoding in normal reading (as opposed to laboratory studies of word recognition) is rarely explained. Many experimental situations leave no alternative to applying spelling-to-sound correspondences because the stimuli include sequences of letters that are either nonwords or only parts of words. Occasional specific justification for the assumption of decoding tends to argue for its necessity for learning to recognize unfamiliar words in the first place (which may be referred to as the "identification problem") or for relieving an assumed memory burden of storing many thousands of unique configurations in the reader's sight vocabulary through some form of phonemic mediation (which may be termed the "recognition problem").

Inside-out theories, on the other hand, tend to ignore or play down the relevance of decoding. They assert that the system of correspondences is extremely complex and of limited reliability for word identification, and that in normal reading situations there are alternative strategies (such as asking someone or using context) that are less time-consuming, more efficient, and already well practised in spoken language learning. For word recognition—the maintenance of a sight vocabulary of familiar words—decoding is regarded as completely unnecessary, since there is no known limit on human memory capacity. Readers of nonalphabetic scripts do not appear to have memory problems, and individuals seem to experience little difficulty in discriminating all the thousands of distinctive objects in their perceptual worlds without the need for mediating systems. Inside-out theories assert that the memory-load argument confuses recognition with reproduction, which is the writer's problem, not the reader's. In a general discussion of all these points (Smith, 1973), it has been argued that the alphabet may function primarily to assist the writer.

The inside-out approach sees as the primary overload problem the fact that the reader may be confronted by too many alternatives: letter combinations "decode" into too many alternative patterns of sound, and many common words have too many alternative meanings and even grammatical functions (e.g., *house*, *chair*, *table*, *empty*, *time*, *narrow*, *open*, *close*). Reducing the number of alternatives in advance by excluding unlikely instances accounts for the absence of awareness of potential ambiguity and also makes spelling-to-sound-correspondence rules effective in practice. This process of employing context and prior knowledge to eliminate alternatives in advance is sometimes termed *prediction* to avoid the educationally loaded term *guessing* by which inside-out theories have sometimes been characterized.

Conflicting Approaches to Reading Instruction

There are also outside-in approaches to reading instruction. Outside-in programs are founded on the general belief that children must first learn the alphabet and then the "sounds of letters" which can be combined to form words that they will recognize (it is hoped) as part of their spoken language. And that, from the outside-in point of view, just about accounts for learning to read. Typically, children who fail to learn to read by such treatment are given more of it.

One reason why outside-in instructional programs are so numerous and widespread in classrooms (and at reading conventions) is that they are a direct reflection of outside-in theories of reading. Outside-in theories "translate" naturally into outside-in instruction. But outside-in instructional programs are also prolific in their own right for the same reason that outside-in theories flourish—they are conceptually simple and lend themselves easily to measurement, manipulation, and control. With outside-in instruction there is little concern with comprehension, either in terms of content or in terms of why the child should be involved in the exercise in the first place. Comprehension of content is supposed to come about automatically if and when the child masters decoding skills, and it is, in any case, the child's responsibility. Comprehension by the child of the purpose of the drills and skills is disregarded; task achievement is everything. And not only are outside-in instructional methods frequently success-ful, within their own limited range of objectives, but they also have the great advantage of being able to demonstrate their success. Objectives can be set within the reach of any desired proportion of a particular population, and scores can be recorded to prove that criterion levels have indeed been achieved. By offering a convenient scale of scores, outside-in procedures will even "diagnose" which children are likely to be good students (i.e., will score high on similar tasks) and which children have "learning disabilities."

The outside-in perspective is a boon to instructional program developers who need to decompose complex tasks into series of discrete and simple steps so that teaching can be standardized and made amenable to technology. To achieve this simplification, a few contemporary reading programs claim to teach only "sub-skills" of reading, relieving the teacher of anxiety about the total skill of which the subskills are a part. Because of their quantitative nature, outside-in procedures are generally adopted whenever someone wants to hold someone else accountable for progress or regression in literacy. Outside-in instruction is usually also the referent when there is concern for "getting back to basics."

Inside-out approaches to instruction, on the other hand, try to argue that children learn to read by reading, and that the teach-er's role is to help children read. Such a perspective asserts that it is sense that enables children to learn to read, making use of inferred meaning and prior knowledge, just as the development of spoken language fluency is rooted in the sense children are able to bring to the learning situation (Macnamara, 1972; Nelson, 1974). According to the inside-out point of view, expecting chil-dren to "decode" letters into words is to expect them to learn words the hard way; it is familiarity with words that makes letter recognition (and phonics) easy. Similarly, the requirement that children should identify strings of words accurately in order to obtain meaning, or without recourse to meaning at all, is also to impose the most difficult task. Anything that does not make sense to children is regarded as a hindrance to their learning. Learning nonsense is not only harder; it is pointless.

The inside-out perspective appeals to the intuitions of many experienced teachers. Their own feelings—often only tentatively expressed because they fear they lack "scientific" validity—are that children learn by being immersed in meaningful written language, in situations that generate pleasure and assurance rather than bewilderment and apprehension. From such a perspective, the more structured outside-in approach may be seen as a systematic deprivation of important information. However, it must also be stated that other teachers are threatened by inside-out points of view, by their lack of structure, the responsibility they seem to throw on the teacher, and the fact that they are not amenable to simple packaging and measurement. They are not labor-saving. They are not explicit about what teachers should do, nor about how student progress would be measured.

Inside-out theories do not offer prescriptions for methodology. They are not directly translatable into practise (Smith and Goodman, 1971). Instead, they aim to inform teachers, to assist them in making their own diagnoses and decisions. Teachers who rely on outside-in instruction need advice, tests, or luck to make appropriate on-the-spot decisions. But the ultimate dilemma for such teachers is that they must still choose. They must select among programs, tests, and experts. And to make such choices they need information, an understanding of the nature of children and of reading. The inside-out perspective does not hold that reading teachers should ignore the tools of their trade, the methods and materials that are available, but it asserts that teachers should know how and when methods and materials are appropriate and when their use may make no sense at all. Inside-out theory can be practical but not by being straitjacketed into programs.

"Interactive" Approaches to Reading

The relevance of prior knowledge and even of expectation in reading has, of course, not been completely overlooked by researchers. However, it is only in recent years that experimental studies have attempted to consider such central factors in a comprehensive and systematic way. Impetus for such studies has come from a perhaps unexpected source—the use of computers to simulate and test hypothesized processes of language and thought. A number of cognitive psychologists and psycholinguists have begun to move away from rather narrowly constrained speculations of how language-based knowledge might be represented in memory to a more elaborate study of reading.

To take just one example, Rumelhart (1977) has characterized reading as an "interactive process" involving a conjunction of "visually derived" and "expectation derived" information. Rumelhart and others have adopted computer terminology to refer to the flow of visually derived information (corresponding roughly to what I have been calling outside-in) as "bottom-up" and to the opposite flow of expectation derived information (my inside-out) as "top-down." Apart from some general background theorizing, however, the studies that have been so far reported have tended to get no farther in (or up) than word recognition and have once more typically allowed subjects little opportunity to demonstrate preferences and strategies they might exhibit in reading outside the laboratory. Visually derived information is still presented to readers for exhaustive analysis of one kind or another, rather than allowing them to sample it selectively for purposes of their own.

One reason why the interactive approach has, in general, been unable to break free of an outside-in bias in experimentation is that it has tended to lean on an extremely narrow conception of comprehension that characterizes computer-based models of language. Inspired largely by "case grammar" linguistic theories (e.g., Chafe, 1970; Fillmore, 1968), such models have been inclined to regard comprehension as a kind of abstract representation (generally in the form of a network of relations) of all the information contained within the structure of an "input sentence." For example, the "meaning" of a sentence such as "My sister is visiting us" would be represented by a logical argument of the form:

RELATION: visit;   SUBJECT: my sister;   OBJECT: us

Since comprehension is assumed to consist of the construction of such an abstract representation, the adequacy of the representation (and of the model) is tested by whether particular parts of the input sentence can be retrieved in response to questions. For example, comprehension of the preceding sentence would be demonstrated if the element "your sister" could be retrieved in response to the question "Who is visiting us?"

However, such formulations are far from competent to handle the fact that comprehension of statements is rarely a matter of being able to regurgitate or even paraphrase what has just been said or read; instead, it depends largely on the receiver's purpose in attending to the statement in the first place. For example, as a response to the question "Could you put me up for a few days?" the statement "My sister is visiting us" means only one thing— no—and it would normally be comprehended in that way. Put more generally, speakers and writers do not normally produce statements in pointless context-free isolation, but with respect to an actual or assumed common interest on the part of both producer and receiver. The actual meaning to both parties is largely determined by factors extrinsic to the statement—namely, the situation in which it is uttered and the prior knowledge and mutual expectations of the two parties concerned. Comprehension is basically a matter of getting answers to questions implicitly asked by the recipient of a message. The ability to paraphrase an utterance or to recall parts of it is no indication of comprehension at all. Yet parsing or paraphrasing are generally the most that computer models of comprehension aspire to achieve, and until further progress is made in the enormous enterprise of trying to represent human knowledge and intentionality in these models, it is unlikely that they will provide a basis for theories of reading that are representative of normal reading situations. Until interactive approaches break free of their dependence on outside-in experimentation and enrich their theoretical foundation with respect to comprehension, expectation that they might have productive implications for classroom practice or instructional development would seem to be premature.

Directions for Further Research

For a start, it would be pointless to expect a critical experiment to determine whether outside-in or inside-out theories are correct. The data are rarely in contention, and the interpretation placed on them depends on one's theoretical proclivity. The issue is a pragmatic one, deciding which particular theories are the most useful for specific purposes, whether those purposes are predicting response latencies in letter- or word-recognition studies, providing an intuitively appealing model of reading, generating worthwhile practical consequences in classrooms, or stimulating productive research. Obviously, all theories of reading and of reading instruction require improvement and offer ample potential for research, but there is a particular need for more robust theories to stimulate research beyond the current rather tired experimental preoccupation with word identification and the seemingly endless and inconclusive comparisons of scraps of instructional technology. In particular, a better understanding is required of how and why children learn to read in the first place, and it is unlikely at present that such an understanding will come from rigorous experimentation under controlled laboratory conditions. There is a dearth of observational information capable of throwing light on the intellectual, emotional, and social needs that reading satisfies, or on why learning to read is often resisted. There is a need for more information about the manner in which children respond to print long before they receive any formal instruction and about the amount and nature of print in the world around them, analogous to the studies of development of spoken language in infants. Very few studies of reading development have been conducted that have not been contaminated by the effects of early instruction. Few studies have been concerned more with children's developing awareness of print than with their ability to cope with the demands and terminology of particular instructional methods.

Further pursuit of a universal method of teaching reading might appear pointless. A mass of existing research demonstrates that all methods of reading instruction achieve certain aims some of the time, although no method has been found to work all the time. Millions of children have learned to read with procedures and materials that are the same as those with which other children have failed. There is, in fact, no evidence that children who are motivated to learn to read experience difficulty in learning to read. And despite the millions of dollars spent on program development and testing by government agencies and commercial enterprises, there is not the slightest evidence that children who succeed in learning to read today do so with any more facility than those who learned with a hornbook and the family Bible.

More consideration must be given to the possibility that literacy problems will not be ameliorated by better descriptions of language or of cognitive processes. For example, a largely neglected theoretical issue that may play a considerable role in the apparent inadequacy of much of our reading instruction is the fact that language as it is normally encountered and employed outside the classroom has a variety of functions (Halliday, 1973). Children do not begin life by learning "language skills" as such; they are never engaged in a purely linguistic exercise. The language they first hear and use always has a function, and language and function are probably learned simultaneously. Children learn to talk while learning that language can be used to satisfy needs, express feelings, explore ideas, ask questions, obtain answers, assert oneself, manipulate others, and establish and maintain specific interpersonal relations. However, children may have acquired ability in one or two functions of language without being able to comprehend all its functions. Sometimes it may be thought that children lack language ability when they are merely unfamiliar with certain functions.

Language in school must often seem to children to have some very odd functions. Sometimes it is used without any obvious function at all—for example, when children are expected to attend to isolated words on chalkboards, meaningless sequences of words in books, and obscure exercises and drills. Schools may attempt to suppress entirely, both in teachers and in children, some functions of language that children find most important. There is very little theorizing and research on these issues, yet as far as literacy is concerned, they may have the most profound implications of all.

Concluding Comments

There are two other reasons why I feel caution should be exercised before acceding to the constant demand for theorists to be "practical" and for the translating of research into practice. The first is that the direct conversion of theoretical insights into practical terms—whether on the level of helpful hints to individual teachers or as full-blown instructional programs—tends to lead to egregious overgeneralization. What might be a good idea with a few children in a limited context becomes inflated into a foolproof system for teaching entire populations the whole time. Teachers who rely on experts rather than on their own accumulated wisdom and experience to solve day-to-day classroom problems become even more disappointed and disillusioned with the theorist or researcher when the desired improvement so rarely comes. More recognition should perhaps be given to the value of theories that assist teachers in making their own decisions.

My second concern is that the rush to translate theory into practice frequently confuses what a person is able to do as a consequence of being a reader with what is necessary in order to learn to read in the first place. A recent example was the effort to transmogrify large numbers of children into transformational grammarians when linguists discovered that transformational rules were a convenient way of characterizing part of their own language competence. Almost contemporaneously, many children were drilled in the identification of meaningless "distinctive features" as a preliminary to exposure to the alphabet, after theorists hypothesized that feature detection models might be a useful conceptual tool for examining letter- and word-recognition processes. Following recent theoretical interest in the roles of redundancy and prediction in reading, there have been attempts to develop programs for teaching children to become responsive to redundancy and to predict, although such abilities are integral parts of the natural capacity of all children to make sense of spoken language long before they get to school.

No theory of reading is likely to be of substantial utility in education unless it reminds teachers and researchers alike that the skill of reading remains largely a mystery because so much of it is embedded in the complex structures and functions of the brain. To discover why some children succeed and others fail we must understand more about what transpires in their heads as they strive to make sense of reading and reading instruction.

8
The Language Arts and the Learner's Mind

There is widespread concern about how the "language arts"—reading, writing, speaking, the comprehension of speech, and possibly also the appreciation of literature—should be integrated in the school curriculum. But there is a more fundamental question of how these different aspects of language must be brought together in the learner's mind. The problem is not one of defining terms (it is hard enough for a teacher to say what precisely constitutes reading, writing, and so forth, except as particular activities in classrooms) but of relating the activities that go under these labels to everything else the learner can understand and do. Unless the various aspects of language, and our efforts to teach them, are integrated in the learner's understanding, then there will be no useful learning in any case.

The categories of the language arts are arbitrary and artificial; they do not refer to exclusive kinds of knowledge or activity in the human brain. Reading, writing, speaking and understanding speech are not accomplished with four different parts of the brain, nor do three of them become irrelevant if a student spends a 40-minute period on the fourth. They are not separate stages in a child's development; children do not first learn to talk, then to understand speech, then to read, and then to write (or any variation of that order). And the four aspects of language do not require different "levels" of cognitive development. The labels are our way of looking at language from the outside, ignoring the fact that they involve the same processes within the brain. In the same way a variety of physical activities may be distinctively labelled as standing, sitting, running, jumping, crawling, swimming, skiing, and so on, although all, from the inside, involve the same muscular systems operating in basically similar ways. How does language look from the inside, from the point of view of a child trying to understand and interact with the world as a whole? How does a child perceive language?

I do not believe that language, in any of its manifestations, is regarded as something "different" by children. Children do not learn language differently from the way they learn anything else,

Reprinted with permission from *Language Arts* 56(2):118–125, February 1979.

nor are they motivated to learn about language for different reasons. Indeed, children do not want to learn "speaking," "listening," "reading," and "writing" as isolated skills or as abstract systems; they want to understand the world in a far more general sense and to achieve their own ends in a far more general sense, and the learning of language in any of its external aspects is entirely coincidental. Language only becomes complicated and difficult to learn when it is separated from other, more general, nonlanguage events and activities in the world.

My argument in this paper is that there is only one essential precondition for children to learn about language and that is that it should make sense to them, both in its content and in its motivation. Children come to understand how language works by understanding the purposes and intentions of the people who produce it, and they learn to produce language themselves to the extent that it fulfills their own purposes or intentions. Where language does not make sense, where it has no apparent purpose, not only will children fail to learn from it but they will actively ignore it. This applies from the very beginning of language learning.

Learning about Spoken Language

Research into the language development of infants has tended to concentrate on the language they produce. Thousands of studies have charted infant progression through babbling, one-word utterances, two- and three-word utterances, and the first rudimentary grammars. Far fewer studies have focused on the language that infants understand, although comprehension is always more extensive than production. We can all understand language that we cannot produce. There is a reason for the bias in children's language research; production is easier to measure. It is not difficult to count and categorize children's utterances, but it is almost impossible to quantify the language they can understand. (For the same reason, and just as unfairly, children's language competence at school is often evaluated from how they speak rather than by what they understand.)

How do infants begin to learn about spoken language? The paradox is that in order to learn language they must first understand it. Children do not first learn language as an abstraction or as a "skill" which they then employ to understand what people are saying. They learn language by understanding the purposes to which it is put. Obviously no one can *tell* an infant how language works, or what it can do; children have to find out about language themselves, by *making sense* of it. And this is the way that children learn about the world in general, about everything in their experience—by hypothesizing what must be going on, anticipating what might occur, and observing to see if they are right. Always children learn by relating what is new to what they understand already.

There is only one way children can make sense of the language they hear around them in the home, at play, and on television, and that is by capitalizing on the fact that the language is often closely related to the situation in which it occurs. Children use the situation, including their perceived intention of the person speaking, for clues to what is being said. This is the reverse of how adults normally perceive language. We think language spoken around us describes situations and indicates speakers' intentions. Parents say "Would you like some milk?" if they want to offer their child some milk; they say "Where's the diaper pin?" when they are searching for a diaper pin. But for the infant this relationship between speech and situation can be used the other way. The fact that the parent is offering milk suggests the purpose of saying "Would you like some milk?" The fact that a parent is searching for the diaper pin indicates the probable meaning of "Where's the diaper pin?" There is no need for anyone to tell the child anything. The child can go from the situation to the probable meaning of the statement and from the meaning to the probable language system that produced the statement. Children can even find out if they have made a mistake. If they think mother said "Would you like some coffee?" and father gets up and puts the cat out, they know a mistake has been made, and they can learn.

If language is meaningful, if it is uttered for a purpose, then the situation in which it is uttered permits the child to deduce its probable meaning and to find out whether the deduction is correct. Thus the child can get on with the difficult business of working out the relationship between utterances and their meaning, the rules of language, without direct adult guidance or correction, simply by hearing and *seeing* meaningful language in use.

Halliday (1973) points out that children learn language and its uses simultaneously; the two cannot be separated. The fact that children have mastered language with some uses—particularly to express the interpersonal relations so important in a child's early life—does not mean that the child can comprehend language used for other purposes, especially the more detached, descriptive, impersonal language of school.

But if language has no perceived use, then it will not be learned and cannot be learned; the perceived use is central to the understanding and the learning. Children must understand the intention. If they can see no purpose to an aspect of language, if they cannot see that it makes any difference, they will not attend to it. It is because children are only concerned with the purposes to which language can be put that they grow up speaking language and not imitating the noise of the vacuum cleaner. Children learn language *because it is there*, part of the world around them, and because it makes sense in that world. Language and the rest of the world are inseparable. Babies can no more ignore the language about the milk than they can ignore the milk that comes with it. They will only ignore language that does not make sense, that exists as noise only.

Learning to Speak

While infants are striving, so successfully and apparently effortlessly, to understand the speech around them, they are learning to produce speech that can be understood. And paradoxically again, in order to learn to speak so that they can be understood, they have to be understood apart from the language they produce. To learn to talk, children have to make their intentions obvious.

It is revealing to reflect upon the uses to which small children put their growing competence in language during the first few years of their lives. They do not learn to talk in order to get their needs met; this they can do perfectly well without language. No baby starves or freezes for want of words. Nor do children develop language ability in order to communicate; they do not exhibit a great passion for conveying information that their listeners might not be expected to know. Instead they spend most of their time saying the obvious. They say "There's a pretty cat," "Lookit the big truck," and "Daddy go walk" when they know perfectly well that you see the cat, the truck or father walking. That is the whole point. When the listener knows what the child is trying to say, that listener can directly or indirectly provide feedback for the child: We can say "No, that's a pretty *dog*," or "Yes, daddy *has gone for* a walk," correcting the child's hypothesis about the world and about adult language. If the adult did not understand the infant's purpose in making the remark, the adult could not correct the remark. Therefore, there is no point in a child saying something that has no purpose, where the intention is not obvious, because then there can be no possibility of learning. When the intention is obvious, the child can learn about language and the world.

Children strive to find out more about the world in a very

general and personal sense. They want to understand the world in which they live, the world as it impinges on them, and since they are part of that world—indeed, they are at the center of it—they want to understand themselves and how they make a difference to the world. They want to understand their relationships with other people, but they also want to understand their own powers. Language is a way of acquiring all these understandings; it is not the only way, but is always one possibility. Sometimes language may be the best way to learn—for example, to find out if an object is safe to touch. Sometimes language may be less adequate—for example, to find out if someone really cares for you. But language can always be put to work, provided the intention behind the language is apparent. There is no point in language without a purpose; with meaningless language there can be no comprehension or learning. Children will neither attend to nor willingly produce and practise language which does not seem to have a point. They are only interested in language that is an integral part of the world; language cannot be something that is "different."

Learning about Written Language

Reading and writing are often regarded primarily as school activities, but their roots must lie outside the school. To the extent that school makes something different or unique of reading and writing, the more it will interfere with children's attempts to understand them.

Two aspects of written language must be distinguished where reading is concerned. One is the written language that occurs in books (which is often thought to be the only kind of written language with which "reading," as a school subject, is concerned), and the other is a quite different kind of written language (which frequently does not have a formal grammar at all) which I shall call "signs."[1] By signs I mean almost all of the writing that surrounds almost all children in their homes and in the world around them—the labels on products in kitchens and bathrooms, the signs in streets and shopfronts and department stores, and the print of television guides, catalogs, sports programs, and telephone directories. I want to call all this written language "signs" because it is directly related to the nonlanguage situation around it. The label on the toothpaste tube indicates the contents

---

[1] In later writing, I dropped the word *signs* and referred to such written (and spoken) language as "situation dependent." In contrast, the language of lectures and texts is "situation independent."

of the tube; the sign "footwear" in the store is related to the department in which it occurs; and the print in a television guide or catalog describes a particular program or product. All of this print, in other words, functions in exactly the same way as the spoken language of the home and street which is the basis for children's learning to understand speech. It is part of the world in general, intimately related to the situations in which it occurs, and it can therefore both motivate and guide a child in learning how it works.

There is growing evidence that children at the age of 3, before they are able to read in any formal sense, can be well aware of the purposes of this kind of written language. They can use the situation in which signs occur to hypothesize their probable meaning (Smith, 1976; Ylisto, 1977), just as they have been able to use the situations in which speech occurs to indicate its probable meaning. Readers think the label indicates the contents of the tube, but children can use knowledge of the contents of the tube to indicate the probable meaning of the label and, again, can find out if they have made a mistake. A boy who goes through the door marked "girls" does not need a teacher to correct his reading. Very small children pay attention to the print around them before they are able to read, because print is part of their world and they can discover that it is put where it is for a purpose. Signs are not arbitrary like the pattern of the wallpaper or the decoration on the shampoo bottle. When children can deduce intention behind print, they can hypothesize its probable meaning and learn. They will not disregard print unless they are persuaded that it has no meaning (because it has no obvious purpose) or unless they find that meaning is irrelevant (because they are instructed to concentrate on words, not sense). But if children are unable to perceive purpose in print, they will find it difficult to attend and impossible to learn, no matter how much a teacher urges them to concentrate upon the words on the board or in the book.

In other words, children expect the written language of signs and labels and catalogs to work in exactly the same way as the spoken language they hear around them in the home; they will attend to it for the same reasons and try to understand it in the same way. For them, print is not something that is different, a unique category of experience, but something that serves very general and understandable purposes in predictable ways. There is no difficulty about integrating an understanding of this kind of written language with a child's knowledge of speech, because it works in the same way as the spoken language with which the child is familiar and is understood and learned in the same way.

The written language of stories and newspapers is a different matter because it is not directly related to the situation in which it occurs. This kind of written language, which might be called "text," is related to situations remote in time and place from where it occurs (like a newspaper report of yesterday's hockey game) or even related to situations that are completely imaginary (like stories).

But once again there is a necessity about the written language of texts. Every word in a story or newspaper article is there for a purpose, but now the purpose is related to the content of the story or article in which it occurs. The *context* determines the meaningfulness of each word. You cannot arbitrarily change words in a story any more than you can randomly change signs in a supermarket or the wrappers on candy bars; each word is where it is for a reason. We do not have to understand the reason the words were put where they are when we read a story; we just have to understand the story (at least until we are expected to do more complicated things at school under a heading like "English" or "literary appreciation"). Usually it is only when we fail to understand that we are reduced to asking "What is the purpose of these particular words; what are they doing here?" If children cannot detect a reason for words they are trying to read, if there seems to be no underlying intention, then they are in trouble. And very naturally they are likely to turn their attention away from the text. Why not? They are gaining nothing from it.

The written language of texts does not work in the same way as the print of signs, and written language in any case is not quite the same as speech. (The differences are relatively superficial, but we can always tell if someone is reading aloud rather than speaking spontaneously.) Therefore, a child's ability to learn to read texts will depend on a prior familiarity with written language, which can only be gained by being read to. Being read to, in fact, enables children to see sense in written language, in books and magazines and newspapers, because they can see that it has a purpose. Again, it just becomes assimilated with everything else that they know. Meaningful texts, like meaningful situations, are those in which a child can find clues to possible meaning and evidence that a mistake has been made. When children have to be corrected by someone else—because they do not find the situation sufficiently comprehensible to correct themselves—there is a certain indication that they are engaged in a task that is essentially devoid of purpose and meaning to them, and no learning will take place.

Learning about Literature

Similar considerations apply as children are introduced to literature. Unless they are familiar with the language (and also the general content) of what they are expected to read, they will experience great difficulty in reading. Certainly there will be no enjoyment. The only way to acquire a starting familiarity with the written language of various kinds of literature is to have heard it read aloud. Just as children cannot learn to read and learn subject matter at the same time—one of them must be a base for learning the other—so students will not learn how to read and enjoy literature if they are unfamiliar with the language and conventions of the literature they are trying to read. Learning always involves relating the new to something that is known already.

Provided understanding is possible and there is no undue apprehension about the consequences of making mistakes, children will learn about literature in the same way that they learn about the world in general, and for the same reasons. Literature offers new ways of exploring the world and new worlds to explore, the stuff a child's brain thrives on. Children can immerse themselves in novels, plays, and poetry with the same enthusiasm with which they immerse themselves in the world, and learn accordingly. It is depressing to think how so many children must have suffered, growing up unable to find pleasure, worth, or sense in literature.

Learning to Write

Writing is often considered the final and most difficult aspect of language, partly because it is often not taught—at least not with any great expectation of success—until children appear to have considerable competence in reading and spoken language, partly because writing ability often seems to lag far behind. But apart from relatively trivial aspects of the physical act of writing, such as the fact that small infants find it hard to hold and control a pencil, there is no reason why fluency in writing should not develop concurrently with fluency in other aspects of language. They have the same roots—the urge to make sense of the world and of oneself.

It is worthwhile to ask why so few people write well (compared with the number who can read) and why even fewer seem to enjoy writing. There are two possible explanations. One is that writing is such a difficult and unnatural activity that relatively few people have the years of training and special talent that it requires. The other possible explanation is that writing is a natural and rewarding activity that just about everybody is born capable of learning, but that something goes wrong for many people.

I think the second explanation is more likely, because writing does basically nothing more than speaking does (so there is no reason for it to be thought unique in any way) and because almost all children find the beginning of writing satisfying. They enjoy making marks on paper, they are impressed by its permanence, and they wonder at the power of print, that it can even represent their own name. Teachers know that one of the hardest things to do with a young child's writing is to throw it away; the writing is part of the child. To children, writing can be as satisfying and as natural as singing, dancing, play-acting, painting, and modelling with clay or mud. It is not something different or special; it is not a unique kind of tool.

Perhaps children grow up reluctant to write for the same reason that so many grow up reluctant to sing, to dance, and to play, at least publicly. We become self-conscious about activities that once were spontaneous, and we become too concerned about our own and other people's evaluation of what we do. We are inhibited. Many adults find it difficult to begin to write, because they are afraid they will not do it well or because they will have nothing to say. It is as if they have a school teacher on their shoulder waiting to criticize every word that comes out. They will never write well if they do not write at all, and they are reluctant to write at all for fear they will not write well.

Writing tends to be laborious in any case. It is tiring physically, demands more concentration, and it is slow, perhaps ten times slower than the speed at which we comfortably manage to read, speak, or listen to speech. We can only become proficient at writing by practice, and we can only write proficiently when we write spontaneously and relatively fast (leaving all the cumbersome attention to spelling, punctuation, and neatness to a later draft). Too much of what happens at school, I am afraid, tends to slow writing down. Writing does not become better if we slow down; it becomes harder.

Writing is not simply a matter of putting down on paper ideas that we already have in our heads. Many ideas would not exist if they were not created on paper. Books never exist in an author's head (except as vague abstractions). It is true that authors shape books, but books shape authors, and ideas that never would have seen the light of day are born in this dynamic interaction called "writing." We do not even know what we are *capable* of thinking unless we begin to manifest ideas in some observable way. When ideas are on paper we can do more than just contemplate them; we can work on them, mold and manipulate them, and build up a structure of new thought as complex and rich as a picture built up on canvas by an artist who started with little more than a generalized intention. Writing is truly creative, if we allow it to be.

There is nothing essentially different about writing; it is another way of discovering more about the world, about possible worlds, and about ourselves. Children should find nothing peculiar or exotic about writing; they should come to it as a natural means of expression and exploration like speech, music, play, and art. Children will strive to make sense of writing in the same way they strive to make sense of any activity—through the manner in which it satisfies purposes and achieves intentions.

As long as writing remains a natural and purposeful activity, made available without threat, then children will be willing to practise it and consequently will learn. Writing, then, is inevitably integrated in the learner's mind with every other productive aspect of language and every other worthwhile activity as well. It is only when writing is treated as a special and difficult kind of activity that it can remain separate from everything else, and therefore impossible to understand, in the learner's mind.

Conclusion

Our categories are arbitrary—reading, writing, speaking, and understanding speech. They are useful perhaps in the way we want to organize our schools, but they are not a reflection of a categorization in the learner's mind. The question is not how the language arts should be brought together in the learner's mind but why they should ever be separated. To a child, language and the world must be indivisible.

9
Myths of Writing

Whether writing should be considered to be as natural as speech for anyone to learn and to practise may be the subject of debate. My own view is that every child who can talk has the capacity to learn to write and also to seize upon the possibilities of written language with enthusiasm. But in any case, I think there can be little debate that writing as children are expected to learn and to practise it in many classrooms is a highly unnatural activity, reflecting (or creating) some basic misconceptions about the nature of writing and about the manner in which proficient writers usually write.

Not all teachers harbor all or even many of these misconceptions. Nevertheless I believe the misconceptions are sufficiently egregious both in school and out to warrant their exposure and examination. Many of them constitute handicaps in teachers' own writing as well as in their efforts to teach children how to write.

I shall present and briefly discuss a collection of twenty-two misconceptions—Smith's myths—which I acquired in the course of a recent exploration of writing (Smith, 1982). For display purposes I shall organize my collection into sets of myths about the nature of writing, about how writing is learned, and about how it is practised, concluding with a grand myth about who is able to teach writing.

Myths about the Nature of Writing

1. *Writing is for the transmission of information.* Reality: Two major functions of writing—to create experiences and to explore ideas—are obscured, if not ignored, by the contemporary "information-processing" approach to literacy (Rosenblatt, 1980). Children may not have much new knowledge to convey to other people, but they will use all forms of language, including writing, if they become aware of its potential, to create worlds of experience and of ideas which they can explore personally, enjoy, and perhaps subsequently share with others. A danger of the information-transmission myth is that it focuses attention on how texts are presented from the point of view of a reader (usually one very touchy about minor points of spelling and punctuation) rather than on what the act of writing can accom-

Reprinted with permission from *Language Arts* 58(7):792–798, 1981.

plish for the developing thought of the writer. The writer is overlooked.

2. *Writing is for communication.* Reality: Writing can, of course, be used for communication, but this is scarcely its only or even major value, certainly not for children. The writer is always the first reader and may often be the only one (for diaries, journals, notes, and more extended texts written for the writer's own exploratory or other purposes). Of course, children often like to show what they write—until they become self-conscious about their expression, neatness, punctuation, or spelling errors—but the purpose of this social act is to share their delight or to demonstrate how clever they are, rather than to communicate information. A similar personal motivation is not absent among adults who have their own written creations prominently displayed on staff room notice boards or in professional journals.

3. *Writing involves transferring thoughts from the mind to paper.* Reality: Writing can create ideas and experiences on paper which could never exist in the mind (and possibly not in the "real world" either). Thoughts are created in the act of writing, which changes the writer just as it changes the paper on which the text is produced. Many authors have said that their books know more than they do, that they cannot recount in detail what their books contain before, while, or after they write them. Writing is not a matter of taking dictation from yourself; it is more like a conversation with a highly responsive and reflective other person. Some reasons why writing is so potent in permitting writers to form and develop ideas they might not have otherwise are considered in the discussions of myths 4 and 5.

4. *Writing is permanent, speech ephemeral.* Reality: Speech, once uttered, can rarely be revised, no matter how much we might struggle to unsay something we wish we had not said. But writing can be reflected upon, altered, and even erased at will. This is the first great and unique potential of writing, that it gives the writer power to manipulate time. Events that occurred in the past or that may occur in the future can be evaluated, organized, and changed. What will be read quickly can be written slowly. What may be read several times need be written only once. What will be read first can be written last. What is written first need not remain first; the order of anything that is written can be changed. Such control over time is completely beyond the scope of spoken language or of thought that remains "in the head."

5. *Writing is a linear, left-to-right process.* Reality: Writing can be done in several places and directions concurrently and is as easily manipulated in space as it is in time. Texts can be

constructed from writing done on separate pieces of paper, in notebooks, on index cards or on chalk boards, at the same time that a main draft is being produced. Words and lines can be moved around on a page just as pages themselves can be re-shuffled into different sequences. Writing is a plastic art.

6. *Writing is speech plus handwriting, spelling, and punctuation.* Reality: Every kind of text has its own conventions of form and expression quite different from any kind of speech. The relevant models for writing are how other people write, not how they speak. Spelling, punctuation, capitalization, paragraphing, indentation, word dividing, neatness, and so forth are necessary aspects of the *transcription* required to make written language manifest, though what is sufficient for a writer to produce and explore written experiences and ideas is by no means as detailed or demanding as the intricacy of transcription required by a reader. The transcription aspects of writing need not, in fact, be done by the writer; they can be looked after by a secretary. For all writers, undue concern with transcription can interfere with *composition*, the creative and exploratory aspect of writing which is, of course, its major value to the writer.

7. *A writer is a special kind of person.* Reality: There is no evidence that writers are any more intelligent, sensitive, talented, dedicated, disciplined, or persevering than people who do not write. Writers come from no exclusive kind of background. Some come from large families, some from small; some from rich families, others from poor; some have literate parents, others the reverse; some received family encouragement, others did not. There is only one difference between writers and people who do not write—writers write. This unique difference may be because writers have some rare and as yet undiscovered gene for writing, though I doubt it. An alternative is that all children are born capable of learning to write at least as well as they learn to talk but something goes wrong. What goes wrong could be related to some of the myths that follow.

Myths about How Writing Is Learned

8. *Learning to write precedes writing.* Reality: Both reading and writing can only be learned in the course of reading and writing. Writing may need years of practice to make it fluent and facile (for most of us, this "learning to write" continues all our lives), but the fluency and facility come with writing, not with repetitive and separate exercises and drills. The only difference between children learning to write and more proficient adults is that children need more help; they can write less by themselves.

They need their own writing to be done for them just as they need other people's writing to be read to them. Unless children try to write and receive help in writing, they will have no motivation for attending to "writing" exercises and instruction, they will find such instruction incomprehensible, and they will not read in ways that will help them learn to write. A disastrous consequence of the "learn now, write later" myth is that the "secretarial" transcription aspects of writing are emphasized before the learner has a chance to experience or even understand the composition aspect of being an author. Even as a means of becoming a secretary, this approach is still not an efficient way to learn.

9. *Writing is learned from instruction.* Reality: Not even such transcription skills as spelling, punctuation, or capitalization can be learned from lectures, from reading about them, or from drills. Spelling is too complex to be learned from rules or by memorizing word lists. And the "rules" of punctuation and capitalization tend, like all grammatical explanations, to be circular: "Begin every sentence with a capital letter." "What is a sentence?" "Something that begins with a capital letter." Formal instruction in grammar is necessarily restricted to conventional niceties like subject-verb agreement, which do not constitute a comprehensive or even comprehensible system for enabling anyone to get thoughts on paper. The easiest way to learn to write is to see something you would like to say (or would like to be able to say) being written.

10. *Writing is learned solely by writing.* Reality: No one writes enough, especially at school, to have enough mistakes corrected to learn to write by trial and error. Not even the transcription aspects of writing could be learned in this way, let alone all the subtleties of style and expression. The only source of knowledge sufficiently rich and reliable for learning about written language is the writing already done by others. In other words, one learns to write by reading. The act of writing is critical as a *basis* for learning to write from reading; our desire to write provides an incentive and direction for learning about writing from reading. But the writing that anyone does must be vastly complemented by reading if it is to achieve anything like the creative and communicative power that written language offers.

11. *Most classrooms are reasonable places in which to expect children to learn to write.* Reality: Most professional writers could not write with the physical and psychological constraints under which many children are expected to learn to write in school. Children who attempted to behave the way most adults find

it necessary to behave while writing would probably not be permitted to stay in the classroom. Much of this discrepancy can be attributed to the following myths (unless the myths themselves have been created to justify the conditions existing in many classrooms).

Myths about the Act of Writing

12. *You must have something to say in order to write.* Reality: You often need to write in order to have anything to say. Thought comes with writing, and writing may never come if it is postponed until we are satisfied that we have something to say. Like every other reference to "writing" in this chapter, this assertion of "write first, see what you had to say later" applies to all manifestations of written language, to letters and memoranda as well as to short stories and novels, to poems, plays, and film scripts as well as to diaries, journals, term papers, research reports, and notes for ourselves and for others.

13. *Writing should be easy.* Reality: Writing is often hard work; it requires concentration, physical effort, and a tolerance for frustration and disappointment. The fact that writing is a demanding activity should not discourage anyone from writing, especially children. Many satisfying activities require physical effort and are not necessarily easy, especially in the learning. Children are not strangers to the idea that worthwhile ends may require effort and concentration, which they frequently display in their "play." Only work which seems to have no point or productive outcome is aversive.

14. *Writing should be right the first time.* Reality: Something all experienced writers know that seems to have been concealed from many teachers is that writing generally requires many drafts and revisions to get ideas into a form that satisfies the writer, and that a separate editorial polishing is required to make the text appropriate for a different reader. Part of the power of writing is that it does not have to be right the first time, that drafts can usually be modified or even thrown away. In a few situations, usually contrived ones like examinations, writing may have to be right the first time. But ability to write in this way requires special practice and is the result of considerable experience. Only through freedom to write provisionally most of the time can the facility be developed of producing first drafts in a form reasonably presentable to a reader.

15. *Writing can be done to order.* Reality: Once again, every experienced writer knows that writing is often most reluctant to come when it is most urgently required, yet quite likely to begin

to flow on inconvenient or impossible occasions. Writing to order is not an ability that develops independently of writing in a more spontaneous and unpredictable manner, nor should it be expected to take priority over such writing.

16. *A fixed period of "prewriting" can or should be distinguishable before any writing act.* Reality: The fact that it is difficult to write to order or to be right the first time does not entail that a fixed period of "prewriting time" exists that should be allocated before writing can be expected to occur. On the one hand, much of what is written involves a whole lifetime of preparation—of experiencing, reading, reflecting, and arguing. It is only from a transcription point of view that an author can say that work began on a particular text at a particular time, even if that was the time when a decision to write was made or formal research begun. And many relevant ideas for what we might propose to write come to us when we are not thinking specifically about what we propose to write, perhaps when we daydream or when we are supposed to be thinking about something else. On the other hand, writing itself can be prewriting. As we draft one part of a text, we reflect upon what we might write next or upon what we have written already. The act of writing does not break itself down into neatly identifiable and manageable "steps;" rather, it is a part of all our existence.

17. *Writing is a sedentary activity.* Reality: Little of the reflective or preparatory aspects of writing can or need be performed at a desk, and even the transcription of writing is sometimes more comfortably performed standing up or in other locations. The traditional notion of the writer quietly working at a desk is romantic and unrealistic.

18. *Writing is a silent activity.* Reality: Writing frequently involves making noise, not only to exchange ideas (or feelings) with other people, but to give vent to expressions of exhilaration or frustration. As with myths 15 and 17, the image of a writer attentive to his muse in garret or cell (the stereotype is usually sexual as well as behavioral) is sentimentalized and unrealistic.

19. *Writing is a solitary activity.* Reality: Writing in general often requires other people to stimulate discussion, to provide spellings, to listen to choice phrases, and even just for companionship in an activity that can be so personal and unpredictable that it creates considerable stress. Especially when writing is being learned, there is often a great need for and advantage in people working together on a letter, poem, or story. The ability to write alone comes with experience and is not always easy or necessary.

20. *Writing is a tidy activity.* Reality: Truly creative (or diffi-cult) writing spreads itself all over the writing surface and all over the floor. Writing is messy; it can involve scissors, paste, trans-parent tape, paper clips, staplers, pens and papers of many colors, and more than one working surface (not all necessarily horizontal).

21. *Writing should be the same for everyone.* Reality: All writers have idiosyncracies. Some write best in the morning, some in the evening; some with pen or pencil, some with typewriter or tape recorder; some only in silence, others only in company; some systematically, others irregularly. Most writers have very strong preferences about writing with a particular kind of instrument on a particular kind of paper in particular locations at particular times with particular kinds of physical and psychological sup-port, holding to these supports with a tenacity verging on super-stition. But then, superstition is a characteristic of all high-risk occupations. Steeplejacks and astronauts have their rabbits' feet. Writers put themselves on the line and undertake enterprises without knowing what the outcome will be. Inconvenient though it might often be, writing behavior may have to be idiosyncratic if it is to be engaged in at all.

The Grand Myth about Who Can Teach Writing

22. *People who do not themselves enjoy and practise writing can teach children how to write.* Reality: Anyone who hopes to teach children how to write must (1) demonstrate what writing can do and (2) demonstrate how to do it. A "teacher" who dislikes or fears writing will demonstrate that writing is to be disliked or feared, just as a teacher who is only seen writing comments on children's work, reports for parents, or notes and exercises for classroom activities will demonstrate that writing is simply for administrative and classroom purposes. Children will learn what is demonstrated, and a teacher who perceives writing as a tedious chore with trivial applications will teach just those things.

For most of the myths I have collected I have not attempted to present a means for their eradication. My general feeling (or hope) is that recognition of the myth should be sufficient for most teachers to avoid falling victim to it. But, for the myth of who can teach writing, I want to offer a practical suggestion.

The assertion is that children will learn to write and to enjoy writing only in the presence of teachers (or other adults) who themselves write and enjoy writing. If some teachers do not have these necessary characteristics, then more might be done to bring people who do have them into the classroom, not just the professionals like local authors and journalists but anyone who enjoys writing letters, poetry, or short stories (just as athletic coaches and assistants do not need to be professional athletes themselves, though they are expected to understand and enjoy the sport).

But an additional and even more desirable solution would be for all teachers to learn to become at least moderately keen and competent writers. And for this they should not themselves turn to the exercises and "how to do it" books any more than they should try to educate their own pupils in this way. Teachers should learn the way children should learn, in the mutual effort of writing with a purpose—the primary initial purpose being one's own joy and satisfaction with what is written—and in the delight of reading widely from a writer's perspective. The easiest way for teachers to learn these things in order to teach children in this way is to learn them *with* children, to share the writing activities with the children themselves. In this way, teachers and children alike should be best able to avoid the tyranny of all the myths of writing and, in the process, discover that writing is a natural, attainable, enjoyable, and highly productive way of spending some of one's time.

10
The Unspeakable Habit

We live in an age of outspokenness, when disclosure of once-unmentionable attitudes, proclivities, and private practices is commonplace and even encouraged. Yet one intimate personal habit remains widely concealed, a subject of embarrassment and ridicule, although it is probably universal, extremely useful, an intrinsic part of a full and productive life, and completely harmless to anyone else. I am referring to the unspeakable and largely untalked-of practice of talking to oneself.

Psychologists have shown a remarkable neglect of the conversations that individuals have with themselves, except for Ruth Weir's (1962) classic account of infant-eavesdropping in *Language in the Crib*, and a controversy between Piaget and Vygotsky. Piaget (1959) referred to talking to oneself as part of an outward progression from egocentric thought to socialized speech. From an opposing perspective, Vygotsky (1962) regarded "inner speech" as a transition from external control of an infant's behavior by the language of others to personal and internal speech which is eventually silenced to become "thought." Both seemed to regard talking to oneself as an essentially childish episode.

Yet I doubt if many adults live in a silent world inside their heads, whether or not they make much noise outside. Many of us sing to ourselves, with or without an inner instrumental accompaniment. We whistle, hum, and produce other sound effects. And especially, we talk to ourselves.

I have been casually interested in the subject of talking to oneself for several years. The question that I first asked myself concerned what fluency in writing and fluency in speaking might have in common. Many people speak articulately but find writing difficult. Others write fluently but are reticent in speech. Some, of course, do both, and a few have difficulty in doing either. My question was whether there might be an underlying language fluency that in some people is expressed orally, in others in writing, in some in both modes, and that might possibly exist in some people who neither speak nor write with ease. Could that common factor be talking to oneself?

I was also interested in the silent speech that psychologists call *rehearsal*, a topic relatively well researched (e.g., Lindsay and Norman, 1977) as the basis of the auditory short-term mem-

Reprinted with permission from *Language Arts* 59 (6):550–554, 1982.

ory which enables us, for example, to keep an unfamiliar telephone number in mind until we are able to dial it. But there is another aspect of rehearsal, ignored by researchers, by which we prepare for something we might want to say, sometimes usefully (when we anticipate and even practise our part in an important interview), but sometimes unproductively, in the phenomenon that I call "seminar speechlessness," (when we are so busy contemplating what we might contribute to a discussion that we finish up saying nothing at all). There is also a converse phenomenon when we recapitulate and elaborate upon conversations after the event, rueful as opposed to wishful thinking. I must have inquired informally of at least 100 people and did not find any who did not talk to themselves, usually silently, sometimes aloud, occasionally both, although many were hesitant and even a little shame-faced in admitting it.

More rigorously recently, I asked a group of twenty-nine male and female undergraduate students in an education course at the University of Victoria to fill in cards concerning their talking-to-self habits. The results can be summarized as follows:

Talk to selves   29
Do not talk to selves   0

No test of statistical significance was applied. One subject reported talking to herself aloud but never silently. The others talked to themselves silently and all but three aloud also. One respondent said she set aside half an hour every morning for talking to herself; the others seemed less organized or deliberate about the activity. The following is a summary of the main responses and some general comments, concluding with a few questions for research and for education.

Why Talk to Oneself?

Reasons given by my respondents for talking to themselves can be summarized under the headings of *cognitive, emotional,* and *social.* No respondent gave fewer than four reasons in response to the open-ended question "Why do you talk to yourself, if you do?" and most gave reasons in all three categories.

The most common *cognitive* explanation was that talking to oneself helps in the organization of behavior, from constructing a mental shopping list to planning for the next few days, weeks, or years. One respondent said, "It clarifies things, like writing on paper except it is faster and more convenient." Talking to oneself not only helps in remembering things but also in making decisions—"When shopping, I ask myself 'Do I really need that?'"

All respondents reported silently rehearsing and evaluating language that they might overtly produce in the future, usually in spoken but also in written form. Contrary to the usual pattern, one respondent said she often imagined writing what she subsequently might say aloud. Many reported reading aloud what they or others wrote and making overt or silent remarks to themselves about what they were reading (marginalia in the mind).

Silent rehearsal was often used for specific practical purposes, in preparing for important interviews or examinations, for example. But it was also employed for quite imaginary ends—for conversations or discussions that were unlikely to take place. Nevertheless, such inner speech might still have the general advantage of providing practice and even self-conducted testing in various uses and constructions of language. Similarly, the frequent practice of running over in the head what one wished one had said in the past is not necessarily a waste of time; it may be useful experience for what one wishes to say (or to avoid saying) in the future.

Interestingly, a substantial amount of talking to oneself seems to go on while other people are talking. Such behavior may appear to be impolite if not distracting, but it could also have positive characteristics. It might take the place of actual interruption, and it might also help to sort out what the other person is saying (just as talking to oneself while reading may sometimes play an important part in understanding, evaluating, and remembering what we read). There should perhaps be a distinction between talking to oneself for the laudable purpose of better understanding what someone else is saying and talking to oneself in order to ignore them. It may be relevant that people asked to explain aloud something they have just heard or read usually try to do so by paraphrasing, not by repeating the same words. In other words (to illustrate the phenomenon by employing it), comprehension might in part involve silently paraphrasing what we hear or read.

Sometimes the problem of deciding upon an appropriate course of action presses hard upon us, in which case talking to oneself would appear to be a common reaction, not in order to avoid thinking about difficulties but in order to be able to tackle them. Nearly all respondents mentioned talking to themselves when puzzled, perplexed, or confused in one _way or another, as a means both of planning appropriate behavior and of summoning up the courage to engage in it. In fact, rather than constituting an alternative to behavior, talking to oneself seems often to be the way behavior is initiated, promoting action which might otherwise not be taken, "trying to psych myself up for some awesome task," as one respondent put it.

Talking to oneself when confused can, however, be much more than just an aid to clear thinking, a mental scratchpad. It can also be emotionally supporting. All respondents reported at least one *affective* circumstance when they talked to themselves, ranging from irritation to exasperation, from venting anger against oneself and others to sorrow for the predicaments of others and themselves. They talk to themselves when bored, depressed, or anxious, and also as an antidote to frustration. More positively, they talk to themselves to recapture, extend, or anticipate enjoyable experiences— "like putting on a favorite record or browsing through old photographs." Obviously, talking to oneself can make life more tolerable and richer.

From a *social* point of view, talking to oneself seems to make loneliness and isolation not only more acceptable but more productive. Several respondents mentioned talking to themselves when alone not simply for company or for want of anything better to do but to ease necessary or desirable solitary activities, such as long-distance driving, swimming, and jogging. One respondent asserted that talking to himself helped him through examinations, "like having someone there to encourage me without actually cheating." Thus talking to oneself when alone can be much more than simply a matter of having a wandering mind. It can enable a person to be less dependent upon others—or upon television—in coping with the passage of time, more self-reliant, and thus, paradoxically, more competent socially.

Talking to oneself is frequently associated with other forms of private behavior such as fantasizing and daydreaming, which may be equally as universal, useful, and maligned as talking to oneself. Together they may be an important part of the constructing and practising of the *scenarios* or *scripts* (Schank and Abelson, 1977) that we employ in order to behave appropriately in new situations (in ordering a meal in a restaurant we have not visited before, for example, or in finding our way through an unfamiliar department store). Several respondents gave instances of talking to themselves as part of imagined complex situations, especially where they might be unsure of the most appropriate or desirable way to act.

Some Questions for Research

My general conclusion from the preceding data and analysis is that talking to oneself is a widespread and frequently useful practice which does not deserve the secrecy and disparagement it commonly receives. Talking to oneself accomplishes ends that talking or writing to other people cannot do as well and sometimes cannot do at all. As a consequence, I think there is a great deal that should be learned and reflected upon about the practice.

For example, what is the linguistic nature of inner speech? Does it have the same grammar and vocabulary as social talking? Several of my respondents thought their talking to themselves was "telegraphic" or elliptical (and my own experience is that I am able to compress the silent rehearsal of a 1-hour lecture into 20 minutes). Others thought their private speech involved "larger thought units." What is the form of this compression or condensation; does it involve different skills from those employed in writing or talking aloud?

How is talking to oneself related to "listening to oneself," widely perceived as an important aspect of composition in writing (Murray, 1968)? Oddly, perhaps, only one of my respondents specifically reported "listening" to voices in his head, and he did so deliberately, allowing his mind to "ramble randomly" to observe where it might go. Does such behavior sound bizarre? It reminds me of the probing and waiting for incubated illumination that psychologists have identified as a concomitant of creativity and even of genius (Getzels and Csikszentmihalyi, 1972).

How much talking to oneself goes on? I get the impression that some people talk more to themselves than to other people (although one might not think so from the relative amount of research attention public and private speech receive). Is there a wide variation in the amount that is done?

How similar are the talking-to-self habits of individuals? Do we all do so in the same way, for the same reasons? There is a fascinating issue at the heart of this—how do we learn to talk to ourselves (if it is something that must be learned)? Obviously infants cannot be imitating others, because they do not know that others are doing it.

How much talking to themselves do children do, and for what reasons? More generally, what exactly is the range of functions of talking to oneself, and how do children become aware of them? Is it, as I wondered at the beginning of this paper and of this inquiry, a necessary basis for and even precursor of overt talking and writing? Could it even be richer than either?

While on the question of research, one might ask why talking to oneself is generally so negatively regarded, why people so often ridicule it in themselves and others? Are we afraid of what others might be saying "under their breaths?"

Some of these issues I consider to be quite profound, relating as they do to the fundamental nature of language and thought and to the control of one's own behavior. Is it possible that there are children and adults who do not talk to themselves, or who cannot do so very well (whatever such an expression might mean)? There is a natural concern if children do not learn to talk with other people. Is it possible that some suffer a cognitive, emotional, or social handicap by not being able to talk to themselves?

Some Questions for Education

If talking to oneself could be so useful in so many ways, should it be ignored quite as much as it is in school? I certainly would not want to suggest that we teach children "talking-to-self skills" in the classroom, but should the matter be quite so pervasively ignored? Should we provide opportunities for children to develop and practise talking to themselves, or at least not upbraid or embarrass them when they do so? Is it time for another social revolution, for "talking-to-oneself liberation?"

In her influential book *Talking and Learning*, Joan Tough (1977) suggests a framework for analyzing and assisting children's overt speech. She points out its important functions in self-maintenance (protecting the self and self-interests), in directing one's own behavior, in reporting on present and past experiences, in furthering logical reasoning, in predicting, in projecting oneself into the experiences and feelings of others, and in imagining. All of this Tough regards as critical in the classroom, a basic concern of teachers. And all of it applies also to children's talking to themselves.

I am hesitant to go on record as suggesting that children and teachers spend more time talking to themselves in school (something some teachers might say they do enough already). But aren't there some issues here that should be talked about, if not with others then at least to ourselves?

11
Demonstrations, Engagement, and Sensitivity

How does anyone learn about language? In a recent examination of writing (1982) and a reconsideration of reading and of spoken language learning, I have been struck by the enormous detail and complexity of the language that most individuals learn. Current psychological and educational views of learning, including the hypothesis-testing approach on which I have tended to rely, now seem to me inadequate to account for all the language learning that is achieved. Nor do they explain those occasional difficulties or failures that most people experience with one aspect of language or another—perhaps with spelling, or with certain points of grammar, or with second-language learning—although the individual may have little difficulty with other aspects of language that are intrinsically no less complicated. What we all learn or do not learn with ease varies from one individual to another, and theories of learning should be able to account for this.

First, I shall illustrate aspects of the complexity of the language that most individuals master without apparent effort, although research is lacking on how much language individuals actually learn. Second, I shall briefly outline a revised approach to learning more compatible with how I now feel language is actually learned, although extensive research will be required to substantiate it. In the following chapter I shall consider some implications of the revised approach for classroom practice.

The Conventions of Language

Languages have become what they are by chance and by use. No one ever sat down and "created" any natural language ("mother tongue"). To learn and use language may be natural, and there is probably a purpose for every nuance in language, but the particular forms of a language have developed and persisted unintentionally; they are *conventional* and not predictable to someone who does not already know them.

This arbitrary nature of language becomes apparent if we consider either a specific language or the thousands of languages

Reprinted with permission from *Language Arts* 58(1):103–112, 1981.

that exist in the world and the wide range of their differences.[1]
There is nothing especially natural or even logical about English,
for example, in comparison with Chinese or Greek or any other
language. There is no particular reason why the animal that is
called "chien" in French and "perro" in Spanish should be called
"dog" in English. There is no special logic behind English phonology or grammar, or punctuation; other languages manage
quite well with different forms and structures or even in their
absence. Without knowing a particular language or the history
of its derivation, it is quite impossible to predict or work out
what its conventions will be.

The Nature of Conventions

Conventions are arbitrary but mutually accepted and expected
ways of doing or expressing particular things. They are essentially contracts for doing things in certain ways which could, in
fact, be done quite differently provided the alternative becomes
the expected. For example, every culture with a road system has a
convention for driving on one side of the road rather than the
other. There is no particular logic or advantage about which side
the traffic drives on, provided it is all on the same side. The form
of the convention is a matter of chance or arbitrary choice (or
of consistency with an existing convention which itself became
established by chance) and therefore quite unpredictable. Thus,
to learn a convention you must first discover what it is and how it
works, a necessity that has enormous implications for how language itself is learned.

Conventions are the basis of shared understandings and communication. If you can understand what I have written, it is
because I have anticipated your expectations about the conventions of language that I have employed. While conventions are
not initially predictable, when learned they are used as the basis
for prediction, and prediction is the basis of comprehension.

Cultures (or human brains) seem to abhor free or random
variation and to be ready always to capitalize upon conventions.
Predictability is preferred and exploited. Take, for example, the
fact that every language in the world that has an alphabet also has
a conventional alphabetical order. I can find no logical reason for

---

[1] The relatively few "universals of language" that have been uncovered
(Greenberg, 1963) are concerned primarily with the range from which
phonologies can be drawn and the absence of certain categories of
grammatical construction. In general, they serve only to underline the
immense variety of natural languages within certain general physio-
logical or functional constraints.

the conventional ABC . . . order of the English alphabet except for tradition itself, but there are good reasons for some order to be established and maintained. All our dictionaries and other reference books, not to mention libraries and entire bureaucracies, depend upon the existence of this arbitrary convention. Imagine the disruption if a rebellion against the tyranny of alphabetical order succeeded.

Conventions pervade language, from the sounds and spellings of individual words to the structures of discourse and the "grammars" of entire stories. The greatest and most complex set of conventions in any language lies in its *registers*, in the appropriate way of talking (or writing) on particular occasions depending upon who is talking, to whom, when, and about what. Registers have little to do with grammar and much to do with the way people are expected to communicate with each other. We are all sensitive to them. Children entering school quickly realize that teachers do not (and should not) talk to them the way their parents or friends do, and everyone becomes embarrassed when visiting a different culture to find that they cannot use or respond to the registers the natives employ and expect. Languages are not learned solely from grammar books.

Nonverbal aspects of language are also conventional. There are conventions for how close we may stand to someone when we talk, how often and how long we may gaze into their eyes, and how much (and where) we may touch them, again depending on all kinds of personal and situational factors. Every culture has conventions such as these, but it is not predictable what the particular conventions will be. What is polite in one culture is rude in another. Nothing is neutral; there is no room for free or idiosyncratic variation. With language, every difference makes a difference. And it all has to be learned.

Some Advantages of Conventions

I am making some very strong statements about language. I am saying that there is only one way to say anything, both verbally and nonverbally, in writing as well as in speech, and that to say anything differently is, in effect, to say a different thing. Synonyms and paraphrases are not substitutable for each other. Choice of a particular synonym always says something about the speaker or the speaker's perception of the listener. *Petrol* and *gasoline* may refer to the same thing, but I reveal something of myself if I use one term rather than the other. *Dogs chase cats* cannot replace *cats are chased by dogs* in any meaningful context. The first is a statement about dogs and the second about cats. In context each will be interlocked with other sentences by conventions of cohesion (Halliday and Hasan, 1976), so that one cannot be substituted arbitrarily for the other.

It may be objected that reducing all of language to convention is to deprive it of its productivity and creativity. On the contrary, conventions are economical, maximizing the flexibility of language and its precision. Because the same thing cannot be said in two different ways, every difference permits us to say something different.

Conventions make creativity possible. Breaking convention is permitted—for a good reason. Ignorance is often sufficient reason. Foreigners and children (except perhaps in school) are expected not to know conventions and therefore not to observe them. Sometimes it is an advantage to be regarded as a foreigner for the latitude allowed to unconventional behavior.

Conventions may also be broken intentionally, to achieve something that cannot be achieved by conventional means. Creative writers often do this to say something they feel they cannot otherwise say, like James Joyce with grammar and e.e. cummings with punctuation. Without conventions there could be no unconventionality. The constraints of language in effect offer us boundless opportunities.

The Extent of Conventions

I cannot begin to catalog all the conventions of a language or how much we learn about them, as the amount and the complexity are staggering. Almost universally the extent of this learning is underestimated, as I shall try to demonstrate with the example of spelling. This is not because I regard spelling as a particularly important, substantial, or difficult part of language learning. But spelling conveniently illustrates that proficiency in particular aspects of language is far more complex than it is generally assumed to be and that current theories of learning not only fail to account for how many individuals achieve unexpectedly large amounts of learning but also why others fail.

I have found no research on how many spellings are known by those individuals who would be characterized as "knowing how to spell"—I shall call them "spellers." My estimate is that the total could be as high as 50,000, since that is a low estimate for the number of words in an average spoken language vocabulary, and most spellers (it seems to me) have a spelling for just about every word they know. Of course, some of these spellings may be wrong, but they are probably a small proportion of the total number of known spellings, and the incorrect spellings have themselves probably been learned—there is a persistence about them.

How does anyone achieve the capacity to spell scores of thousands of words, most of them correctly? We do not spell by writing down the sounds of words; the worst spellers are the wuns hoo rite fonetically. But we also do not spell by applying spelling rules. Even if you have learned all of the 300 sound-to-spelling correspondences that can be found in a relatively small sample of 20,000 common English words (Venezky, 1970), your chance of being correct in applying the rules to spell any of those same 20,000 words is slightly less than 50 percent (Hanna, Hodges, and Hanna, 1971). Even if the rules do happen to spell an unknown word correctly for you, you still must inquire whether the spelling is correct, as none of the rules comes with a guarantee. There is only one way for anyone to become a speller and that is to find out and remember correct (i.e., conventional) spellings.

Remembering many thousands of spellings would not appear to be the problem, not for most people at least. The brain usually takes remembering in its stride. We have all remembered the sounds of 50,000 words or more (sounds far more complex and arbitrary than their spellings) and also meanings and rules for the use of all those words, a total that must run into hundreds of thousands since the majority of words have many more than one meaning. Also, of course, we are all capable of remembering astronomical numbers of other things—all the faces, places, animals, objects, events, relationships, and attributes that we find familiar in the world, by sight, sound, touch, taste, and smell.

What must be explained, in spelling and all the other conventions of language, is how an individual finds out and learns what is appropriate in the first place. How could anyone learn the conventional spellings of scores of thousands of English words—one at a time? The answer cannot be formal instruction. The number of word lists that would have to be studied and the limited success that even adept spellers have in learning and retaining items from lists makes it improbable that rote learning explains very much. And I do not think spellers can attribute their success to 50,000 trips to the dictionary or to being told a spelling when they happened to need it.

I was tempted to think that we learn to spell by writing, but that is not an adequate explanation either. Even if children learn a spelling every time a mistake is indicated (and I have found no evidence of *that*), I doubt whether many children write 50,000 words during their school career. Certainly they would not write 50,000 *different* words, and some of the words that we can all spell occur in the language with a frequency of one in a million or less. A check of the Thorndike-Lorge (1944) word list will reveal words with familiar meanings and spellings that we probably encounter only once every 5 years, words we have never written and perhaps not even spoken in our lives.

I can think of only one way in which such an enormous repertoire of spellings might be learned and that is by reading. *We learn to spell by reading.* But now I have problems. Reading may be necessary for learning spellings, but it is obviously not sufficient. Many people read who cannot spell. And I myself have argued that readers need not pay attention to spelling, that indeed it can interfere. How, then, does one account for the enormous amounts of learning that spellers must do when they read, without effort or awareness, and also for the fact that other readers do not learn to spell, though they may learn other equally complex and numerous conventions? Learning theories based upon association, or stimulus-response connections, or on reinforcement seem to me completely inadequate to account for either the learning or the failure to learn, while hypothesis-testing seems equally unsatisfactory. Surely we gain only a small part of our spelling competence by having hypothesized spellings confirmed or corrected. And where do those hypotheses come from?

How do writers learn to punctuate, to capitalize, to produce grammatical constructions? Again, not from formal instruction or rules. Linguists cannot agree upon or even suggest anything like a complete set of the internal "rules"that speakers of a language must respect to generate or evaluate grammatical sentences. And the other type of "rule" that is the common currency of classrooms and textbooks tends to be hopelessly circular: "Always begin a sentence with a capital letter and end it with a period (or question or exclamation mark)." "What is a sentence?" "Something that begins with a capital letter and ends with a period." Rules like "a sentence expresses a complete thought" only appear to make sense when you can recognize a sentence in the first place.

But grammar, punctuation, and capitalization also cannot be learned by trial and error, from writing and correction. Not even professional writers write enough to hypothesize all the possible constructions that they will eventually master, nor are they edited sufficiently to eliminate almost all possible sources of error. I am not arguing that writing does not play a role in learning to write, just as speaking is important for learning to talk. But the *source* of the information that makes us writers and speakers must lie in the language of other people, accessible to us only through reading and in listening to speech.

How and when do we learn it all? The language we know is enormously subtle and complex, and we learn almost all of it without even knowing that we are learning. We do not know what we know. How is all this learning achieved?

The Learning Brain

I can think of only one general explanation for how we manage to learn so much about language (and concurrently about so much else) and that is that the brain is learning all the time. Learning is not an occasional event, to be stimulated, provoked, or reinforced. Learning is what the brain does naturally, continually. It is only in artificially contrived experimental or instructional situations that the brain usually finds itself not learning—and tolerating not learning. (And even then, learning is probably taking place, that such experimental or instructional situations are artificial, unproductive, and boring.)

This is the time bomb in every classroom—the fact that children's brains are learning all the time. They may not learn what we want them to learn. They may not learn what we think we are teaching them. But they learn, if only that what we try to teach them is boring or that they are unlikely to learn what we think we are teaching. Learning is the brain continually updating its understanding of the world; we cannot stop the brain from doing this. The hazard of so much instruction is not that children do not learn, but what they learn.

The important question for researchers is not how we learn, in the sense of the underlying brain processes, but why a brain which normally learns so effortlessly, so continuously, should sometimes be defeated by tasks that are intrinsically not exceptionally difficult. The answer cannot be in the nature of the brain itself, for if it can learn one thing, why not everything? I cannot believe that there are brain cells or structures that specialize in spelling, punctuation, arithmetic, mechanics, physics, botany, or any of those things that many otherwise unexceptional people can learn while other otherwise competent people fail. The answer must have something to do with the brain's approach to learning rather than with any innate and specific inability to learn. It must be possible for the brain to learn in such a way that certain areas of learning in effect become closed off.

This is the point I want to explore under three general headings which I now see as three basic aspects of learning. One aspect is related to the environment, which I shall call "demonstrations"; one to the interaction of the environment and a learning brain, which I shall call "engagement"; and one with the brain itself, which I shall term "sensitivity."

Demonstrations

The first essential component of learning is the opportunity to see how something is done. I shall call such opportunities "demonstrations," which in effect show a potential learner "This is how something is done." The world continually provides demonstrations through people and through their products, by acts and by artifacts.

Every act is a cluster of demonstrations. A teacher who stands before a class demonstrates how a teacher stands before a class, how a teacher talks, how a teacher dresses, how a teacher feels about what is being taught and about the people being taught. A tired teacher demonstrates how a tired teacher behaves, a disinterested teacher demonstrates disinterest. Enthusiasm demonstrates enthusiasm. Not only do we all continually demonstrate how the things we do are done, but we also demonstrate how we feel about them. What kinds of things are demonstrated in classrooms? Remember the time bomb: children are learning all the time. What kind of writing do children see teachers doing? What do teachers demonstrate about their interest in reading?

Every artifact is a cluster of demonstrations. Every book demonstrates how pages are put together, how print and illustrations are organized on pages, how words are set out in sentences, and how sentences are punctuated. A book demonstrates how every word in that book is spelled. What kinds of things do our artifacts in the classroom demonstrate? Is it possible that those continually learning brains are exposed to demonstrations that books can be incomprehensible, that they can be nonsense?

There are some interesting kinds of demonstrations that I do not have space to go into here. I would like to explore *inadvertent* demonstrations. In a sense, most demonstrations are inadvertent, but sometimes we can demonstrate one thing quite unintentionally when we actually think we are demonstrating another. Some simulations may fool ourselves—but those ever-learning brains? An important category of demonstrations is self-generated, like those we can perform in our imagination. We can try things out in the mind and explore possible consequences without anyone actually knowing what we are doing. But imagination has its limitations; it is ephemeral. Writing can offer the advantages of thought and more. It can be private without the disadvantage of transience. We can (in principle, at least) keep writing as long as we like and manipulate it in any way we like to demonstrate and test all kinds of possibilities, without the involvement of other people.

The world is full of demonstrations, although people and the most appropriate demonstrations may not be brought together at the most appropriate times. And even when there is a relevant demonstration—for example, a spelling that it might be useful for us to know—learning may not take place. There has to be some kind of interaction so that "This is how something is done" becomes "This is something I can do."

Engagement

I use the term *engagement* advisedly for the productive interaction of a brain with a demonstration, because the image I have is of the meshing of gears. Learning occurs when the learner *engages* with a demonstration, so that it, in effect, becomes the learner's demonstration. I shall give two examples of what I mean.

Many people are familiar with the experience of reading a book, magazine, or newspaper and stopping suddenly, not because of something they did not understand, but because their attention was taken (engaged?) by a spelling they did not know. They did not start to read to have a spelling lesson, nor could they have predicted the particular unfamiliar spelling that they would meet, but when they encountered it—perhaps a name they had only previously heard on radio or television—they stopped and in effect said "Ah, so that's the way that word is spelled." At such a moment, I think, we can catch ourselves in the act of learning. We have not simply responded to a spelling; we have made it a part of what we know.

The second example is similar. Once again we find ourselves pausing while we read, this time not because of a spelling and certainly not for lack of understanding, but simply because we have just read something that is *particularly well put*, an interesting idea appropriately expressed. This time we have engaged not with a spelling or even with a convention of punctuation or grammar, but with a style, a tone, a register. We are learning vicariously, reading as if we ourselves might be doing the writing, so that the author's act in effect becomes our own. This, I think, is the secret of learning to write by reading—*by reading like a writer*.

The two examples I gave were necessarily of situations in which we might actually be consciously aware of a learning moment. But such moments are, I think, rare. Perhaps we catch ourselves engaging with a new spelling because it is a relatively rare event, as most of the spelling we need to know we know by now. Children learning the sounds, meanings, and spellings of scores of new words every day of their lives are hardly likely to be stopped, like an adult, by the novelty of actually meeting something new. Instead, most of their learning must be like adult learning from the newspapers and the movies, an engagement so close and persistent that it does not intrude into consciousness.

We engage with particular kinds of demonstrations because "that is the kind of person we are," because we take it for granted with our ever-learning brain that these are the kinds of things we know. My explanation may sound simplistic, but I can think of no alternative. Obviously we can learn by doing things ourselves. With engagement we assimilate the demonstration of another (in an act or artifact) and make it vicariously an action of our own. What I still must account for is what makes us the kind of person we are; what determines whether or not engagement takes place.

Sensitivity

What makes the difference whether we learn or do not learn from any particular demonstration? I thought at first that the answer must be motivation but have decided that motivation is a grossly overrated factor, especially in schools where it is used to cover a multitude of other possibilities. For a start, learning of the kind I have been describing usually occurs in the absence of motivation, certainly in the sense of a deliberate, conscious intention. It makes no sense to say an infant is motivated to learn to talk, or that we are motivated to remember what is in the newspaper, unless the meaning of motivation is made so general that it cannot be separated from learning.

On the other hand, motivation does not ensure learning. No matter how much they are motivated to spell, or to write fluently, or to learn a foreign language, many people still fail to learn these things. Desire and effort do not necessarily produce learning. Indeed, the only relevance of motivation to learning that I can see is (1) that it puts us in situations where relevant demonstrations are particularly likely to occur and (2) that learning will certainly not take place if there is motivation *not* to learn.

My next conjecture was that expectation is what accounts for learning. We learn when we expect to learn, when the learning is taken for granted. This, I think, is closer to the truth, but a *conscious* expectation is not precisely what is required. Infants may take learning to talk for granted but not in the sense of consciously expecting it. Rather, what seems to make the difference is absence of the expectation that learning will not take place.

This is how I propose to define *sensitivity*, the third aspect of every learning situation: the absence of any expectation that learning will not take place or that it will be difficult. Where does sensitivity come from? Every child is born with it. Children do not need to be taught that they can learn; they have this implicit expectation which they demonstrate in their earliest learning about language and about the world. Experience teaches them that they have limitations, and unfortunately experience often teaches them this unnecessarily. Children believe their brains are all-potent until they learn otherwise.

Why is learning to talk generally so easy whereas learning to read is sometimes so much harder? It cannot be the intrinsic difficulty of reading. Infants learning to talk start with essentially *nothing*; they must make sense of it all for themselves. Despite the remarkable speed with which they are usually credited with learning about language, it still takes them 2 or 3 years to show anything approaching mastery. Reading should be learned very much quicker, as it has so much spoken language knowledge to support it. And when children do learn to read, whether they learn at 3 years of age, 6, or 10, they learn—in the observation of many teachers—in a matter of a few weeks. The instruction may last for years, but the learning is accomplished in weeks. What is the difference? I can only think that, with reading, there is the frequent expectation of failure communicated to the child, so often self-fulfilling.

Why is learning to walk usually so much easier than learning to swim? Walking must surely be the more difficult accomplishment. Infants have scarcely any motor coordination and on two tottering feet they must struggle against gravity. Little wonder walking takes several months to master. Swimming, on the other hand, can be learned in a weekend—if it is learned at all. It is learned when the learner has much better motor coordination and in a supportive element—water. And it must be as "natural" as walking. So why the difference? Could it be that difficulty and failure are so often anticipated with swimming and not with walking?

The apparent "difficulty" cannot be explained away on the basis of age. Teenagers are expected to learn to drive cars—surely as complicated a matter as learning to swim, if not to spell—and lo, they learn to drive cars. In fact, for anything any of us is interested in, where the learning is taken for granted, we continue to learn throughout our lives. We do not even realize we are learning, as we keep up to date with our knowledge of stamp collecting, astronomy, automotive engineering, spelling, world affairs, the television world, or whatever, for the "kind of person" we happen to be.

Engagement takes place in the presence of appropriate demonstrations whenever we are sensitive to learning, and sensitivity is an absence of expectation that learning will not take place. Sensitivity does not need to be accounted for; its absence does. Expectation that learning will not take place is itself learned. The ultimate irony is that the brain's constant propensity to learn may in fact defeat learning; the brain can learn that particular things are not worth learning or are unlikely to be learned. The brain is indiscriminate in its learning—the time bomb in the classroom—and, like the incorrect spelling, it can learn things that it would really do much better not learning at all. Learning that something is useless, unpleasant, difficult, or improbable may be devastatingly permanent in its effect.

If this is true, what is the consequence of all the tests we give at school, especially on the children who do not do so well on them? What is the effect of "early diagnosis" of so-called language problems, except to transform a possibility into a probability? Children's brains are not easily fooled. They learn what we demonstrate to them, not what we may hope and think we teach.

Conclusion

The human brain learns all the time. But in the process of learning particular things, or even before the learning of those things has begun, the brain may learn that these things are not worth learning, or are unlikely to be learned. Everyone concerned with practice and research in education should perhaps develop more sensitivity to the nature of the demonstrations with which children might become engaged in school.

12
The Choice Between Teachers and Programs

In Chapter 11, I discussed the proposition that children's brains learn constantly. Everything demonstrated by children by act or by artifact is likely to be learned by them. Educators should not ask why children often do not learn what we believe they are taught, but rather what they might be learning in its place. Teachers may not teach what they think they are teaching.

In the present article I shall consider some implications of the view that children are always likely to learn what is demonstrated to them. In particular I shall argue that the critical question confronting teachers of language arts today is not how writing, reading, and other aspects of literacy should be taught, but what we want children to learn. This is not a question for research to resolve; the relevant evidence is available. Rather, the question requires a decision, upon which the future of teachers and of literacy may depend.

The decision to be made is whether responsibility for teaching children to write and to read should rest with people or with programs, with teachers or with technology. This is not a matter of selecting among alternative methods of teaching children the same things. Different educational means achieve different ends (Olson and Bruner, 1974). The issue concerns who is to be in control of classrooms, the people in the classroom (teachers and children) or the people elsewhere who develop programs. Different answers will have different consequences.

The argument will cover the following points: (1) that programs cannot teach children literacy (though they may be extremely efficient at teaching other things); (2) that programs and teachers are currently competing for control of classrooms; and (3) that teachers will lose this contest if it is decided in terms of those things that programs teach best. Of course, I must be more explicit about what I mean by "programs." But first I shall briefly restate some relevant points from the previous chapter.

The Ever-Learning Brain

Analysis of the enormous complexity and essential arbitrariness of the conventions of language that all children master who

Reprinted with permission from *Language Arts* 58 (6):634–642, 1981.

succeed in using and understanding the familiar language used around them led to the proposition that children's brains strive to learn all the time. Children cannot tolerate situations in which it is not possible for learning to take place. Boredom or confusion are as aversive to brains whose natural and constant function is to learn as suffocation is to lungs deprived of the opportunity to breathe.

Learning occurs in the presence of *demonstrations*, and what is learned is whatever happens to be demonstrated at the time (or rather, the learner's interpretation of the demonstration, the way the learner makes sense of it). Learning never takes place in the absence of demonstrations, and what is demonstrated is always likely to be learned. Demonstrations are continually and inevitably provided by people and by products, by acts and by artifacts. A teacher bored with what is being taught demonstrates that what is taught is boring. A reading or writing workbook containing nonsensical exercises demonstrates that reading and writing can be nonsensical. Demonstrations can also be self-generated; they can be constructed by imagination and reflection in the privacy of the mind.

Learning is an interaction, a concurrent event rather than a consequence of a demonstration. Learning is immediate and vicarious, the demonstration becoming in effect the learner's own learning trial. I term this interaction *engagement* to indicate the intimate meshing of the learner's brain with the demonstration.

Engagement with a demonstration will occur if there is *sensitivity*, defined as the absence of expectation that learning will not take place. The expectation that learning something will be difficult, punishing, or unlikely is itself learned and can be devastating in its long-term consequences. Like all other learning, the expectation that learning will not occur is established by demonstrations.

To learn to read and to write, children require (1) demonstrations of how reading and writing can be used for evident meaningful purposes, (2) opportunities for engagement in such meaningful uses of reading and writing, and (3) freedom from the unnecessary undermining of sensitivity. Obviously teachers are able (or should be able) to provide such demonstrations and opportunities for engagement. The question is whether programs can also meet the three requirements.

The Nature of Programs

Programs appear in a number of educational guises—as sets of materials, workbooks, activity kits, guidelines, manuals, record sheets, objectives, television series, and computer-based instructional sequences. The history of instructional programs is probably as long as that of education itself, but they began proliferating during the present century as experts in other fields (such as linguistics, psychology, computer science, and test construction) and other external agents increasingly asserted views about what and how teachers should teach. The assumption that programs could achieve educational ends beyond the capacity of autonomous teachers grew rapidly in North America with the educational panic that followed Sputnik in 1957 and the coincidental development of management systems and operational techniques for the solution of such logistical problems as sending people to the moon. The pervasiveness of programmatic approaches to education is now expanding further and faster as the development of microcomputers makes a new technology available for the delivery of prepackaged instruction.

Despite their manifold variety in education, programs have a number of common elements, the most critical being that they transfer instructional decision-making from the teacher (and children) in the classroom to procedures laid down by people removed from the teaching situation by time and distance.

Children and teachers can be programmed in the same way that computers are programmed, with all goals and activities specified in advance and procedures provided for every decision to be made. Unprogrammed decisions made by computers are regarded as random behavior likely to divert or derail the entire program, and the same attitude is taken in the programming of teachers and children. At least one commercial reading program specifically admonishes teachers not to answer questions asked by children which the program has not anticipated. Some programs are explicitly "teacher-proof"; others merely warn teachers not to improvise or to tamper with their procedures. No program, however "individualized," asserts: "This program should only be used by a sensitive and intelligent teacher capable of exercising independent judgment about whether it makes sense to use this program with a particular child on a particular occasion." Instead, there is an assumption that the program will be more sensitive and intelligent than the teacher, that instructional decisions will be better made in advance by individuals who do not know and cannot see the child who is supposed to be learning from the program (and who in turn cannot see, know, or question them).

Educational programs share a number of other characteristics, all deriving from the fact that they strive to make decisions in advance on behalf of teachers and children. All of these common characteristics constitute constraints or limitations on what the program can achieve, yet paradoxically they are frequently claimed to be virtues of the program. For example, it is a critical limitation of programs that they cannot demonstrate what reading and writing are for. Teachers can demonstrate the utility of literacy by ensuring that children observe and participate in written language activities that have a purpose—stories to be written and read for pleasure, poems to be recited, songs to be sung, plays to be acted, letters to be sent and received, catalogs to be consulted, newspapers and announcements to be circulated, advertisements to be published, signs to be posted, schedules to be followed, even cribs to be concealed, all the multiplicity of ways in which written language is used (and taken for granted) in the world at large. None of these purposes can be demonstrated by programs, which can only demonstrate their own instructional intentions. Reading and writing are *human* activities, and children learn in the course of engaging in them. Programs must assume that children will learn to read and write before actually engaging in these activities, which means that programs demand learning for which no utility is evident.

The virtue claimed for programs in face of the fact that their instruction is decontextualized and bereft of evident purpose is that they are "skill-based," that they teach basics or subskills with an implied promise that isolated fragments of skill and knowledge will one day fall into place and the learner will suddenly become able to participate in the new and hitherto unexplored activities of reading and writing. Because programs are more concerned with exercises than purposes, their activities bear little resemblance to any normal, motivated, selective act of reading or writing. Therefore, program developers tend to depend on theories that reading and writing are inherently unnatural and difficult (e.g., Mattingly, 1972; Liberman and Shankweiler, 1979), to be learned by rote rather than by the meaningfulness which is the basis of spoken language learning.

All programs fractionate learning experience. Because learners cannot be left free to wander at will through (and out of) the program—which would then not be a program—tasks have to be broken down into small steps without evident relationships to each other or to reading and writing as a whole. Because learners can have no intrinsic motivation to perform such tasks—there is no evident reason for doing one thing rather than another—the order in which tasks must be approached and mastered is narrowly prescribed. This is totally unlike the way in which infants are immersed in the environments of meaningful spoken language, to be progressively understood in the manner that makes most sense to each individual child. The virtue claimed for the highly artificial and arbitrary sequencing of programmatic learning is that it is systematic and scientific, although it could equally well be characterized as a systematic deprivation of experience. The responsibility assumed by prescribing the exact nature and order of experience that each individual child requires in order to reach an understanding of reading and writing is awesome, analogous to restricting a child's exploration of the visual world to glimpses of predetermined events paraded past a slit in an enveloping curtain.

Also because of the purposeless and decontextualized nature of programmatic instruction, the program itself must decide whether the learner is right or wrong. When language is employed for meaningful uses, the context provides clues that indicate not only what the language is probably about and how it works but also whether the learner is right or wrong. There are only two kinds of mistakes in such meaningful language, those that make a difference and those that do not. A mistake that does not make a difference does not make a difference. A mistake that makes a difference becomes self-evident and is the basis of learning. But with meaningless programmatic instruction, every deviation from the literal path is an "error" although the only difference it can possibly make is that it is not permitted by the program. Mistakes are to be avoided rather then accepted as opportunities for learning. Nevertheless, learners are constantly moved toward difficulty because tasks that they can accomplish without error are regarded as "learned" and no longer relevant. The virtue claimed for these constraints is that learning can be promoted, monitored, and evaluated every step along the way. There is "quality control" of both the learner and the teacher, no matter how insignificant the mistake or irrelevant the learning task.

As programs have become increasingly more systematic, greater restrictions have been placed on both the time and possibilities available to teachers to introduce activities of their own. Programs dominate classroom activities. The virtue claimed for this limitation is that programs become total "management systems" for delivering instruction to children. Instruction is seen as a manufacturing process, with the learner as raw material, the teacher as tool, instruction as "treatment," and a literate child as the product delivered at the end. Few program developers are as frank as Atkinson (1974), who admitted that his own elaborate computer-based program began with phonic drills because these could be most easily programmed on the computer. The importance of comprehension in reading (but not in learning) was acknowledged by the characteristic programmatic strategy of treating comprehension as a set of skills to be acquired rather than a state which is the basis of all learning.

Because programs are, by their very nature, piecemeal, unmotivated, standardized, decontextualized, trivial, and difficulty-oriented, it would often not be apparent what they were supposed to be teaching if this were not clearly indicated. Teachers often say they are teaching reading or writing (or spelling or comprehension) because this is the label attached to the program that happens to be in use. And programs are typically not modest in their claims, particularly those that insist upon being the most rigorous. A widely promoted program of "direct instruction" claims that "any child can learn if he's taught in the right way," the right way being the "carefully developed and unique programming and teaching strategies" of the system. To continue quoting from the promotional materials, "The teacher knows exactly what she has to teach. And how to teach it. All the steps for presenting a task, evaluating student responses, praising and correcting the children are carefully outlined." Having made every decision in advance, including when it is appropriate to praise, the program claims that "the teacher can concentrate fully on teaching," though what is left to be taught (apart from the program) is not specified. A more frankly commercial program combines mutually incompatible vogue words with hyperbole to claim that "The needs of the gifted, the average and the perceptually handicapped child are all met through (the program's) psycholinguistic approach. . . . Pupils are introduced to reading through the multisensory-motor method . . . combined with intensive audiovisual activity." Also not untypically, this program claims to be indebted to eminent neurologists who had emphasized "the central role played by the integrative areas of the brain" and "the functional grouping of neural units in learning," as if the activities laid down in the program had some kind of unique neurophysiological status.

The Relevance of Research

Another egregious characteristic of programs in education is their claim to be based upon research. The more elaborate and restrictive the program, the more its developers are likely to assert that its content and successes are validated by empirical evidence while instruction that is based on teacher insight and experience is likely to be dismissed as naive, intuitive, and primitive. "Child-centered" is used as a derogatory label.

However, despite all the claims and assumptions, there is no evidence that any child ever learned to read because of a program. And probably there never could be such definitive evidence, because no child (one would hope) is ever exposed to a "controlled" situation of only programmatic instruction without other access to written language in its manifold purposeful manifestations in the world. On the other hand, there is abundant empirical evidence that children have learned to read without the benefit of formal instruction, either before they came to school or by interaction with teachers who were independently self-directed (Clark, 1976; Torrey, 1979). Often such children have few social or intellectual advantages; they are precisely the children for whom programmatic instruction is supposed to be particularly appropriate.

Research has yet to look closely at the manner in which children frequently learn to read and write without or despite formal instruction, nor indeed at what children actually learn as a consequence of such instruction. Instead research has tended to concentrate only on whether children learn whatever fragmented skills particular programs happen to teach. The research paradigm often contrasts an experimental group that receives a particular program with a "control" group that does not. Both groups are then tested on the specific instruction, and the experimental group naturally does somewhat better. Alternatively, one program is compared with another, generally to show minimal difference between them (Bond and Dykstra, 1967; Stebbings et al., 1977; House et al., 1978). The advantage of whatever such programs actually teach seems to wash out after Grade 3 (Williams, 1979; Chall, 1967) when matters of comprehension begin to assume inescapable proportions.

Considerable research remains to be done on how, exactly, children succeed in learning to read and write, but it will not be done by researchers who believe that such learning is a matter of mastering programmatic reading and writing skills. Instead, there is a great need for longitudinal and ethnographic studies of how children come to make sense of print and its uses, such as those of Goodman (1980), Ferreiro (1978), and Heibert (1981), demonstrating, for example, that preschool children can understand functions and the general character of print long before they receive formal instruction.

Much more research could be done into what children can and

must learn about reading and writing without recourse to programs, into how programs do and should relate to this prior knowledge, into what teachers who succeed in helping children learn to read and write actually do, into what exactly children who have learned to read and write have learned (from teachers and from programs), and also into what children who have failed to become readers and writers have learned. On the other hand, the fact that research demonstrates particular skills that non-readers do not have should not be interpreted to mean that non-readers will become readers if drilled in those particular skills, which may be a consequence rather than a cause of reading. Such has been found to be the case for knowledge of letter names (Samuels, 1971) and for familiarity with the conventional language of reading instruction (Downing and Oliver, 1973–74).

Teachers Versus Programs

With their inevitably limited objectives, programs teach trivial aspects of literacy and they can teach that literacy is trivial. Children are learning all the time. Rather than demonstrate the utility of written language, programs may demonstrate that reading is nonsense and ritual, that writing is boring, that learning is threatening, that children are stupid, teachers are puppets, that schools cannot be trusted, and that children's own interests, cultures, and insights into language can be ignored. Teachers can demonstrate all these things too, but programs do so more efficiently.

The proliferation of programs in education today is unnecessary, irrelevant, and dangerous. Programs are unnecessary, because millions of children have learned to be literate without the contemporary technology of instructional development and there is no evidence at all that the employment and enjoyment of literacy have increased with the growing reliance upon programs. There is no evidence that children who have difficulty becoming literate do better with impersonal programs (although they may exhibit irrelevant and limited learning from what the programs teach). Rather, it is the children who have the least success in learning who most need personal contact, to be reassured of their ability to learn and of the utility of what is to be learned. I am not saying that teachers cannot, on occasion, make independent use of material provided with programs, but that teachers should not be used by programs.

Programs tend to be irrelevant by their very nature. They demonstrate tasks rather than purposes. There is widespread anxiety today because many students leave school with poor writing and reading abilities. But the real tragedy is that competent readers and writers as well as the less able leave school with a lifelong aversion to reading and writing, which they regard as purely school activities, as trivial and tedious "work." Students of weak ability who are interested in reading and writing will always have the hope of improvement. But those who detest the activities are lost; they have learned from the wrong demonstrations.

Programs are dangerous because they may take the place of teachers. The issue is more critical today than ever before because more people seem to believe that the way to improve education is to operationalize it even further and because the technology now exists to make teachers redundant. It is widely(believed, especially among those who promote computer-based instruction, that children can "do all their learning" at a console, that microcomputers are cheaper than teachers (which is a fact) and that they are more efficient than teachers (which is true for what such devices teach best). It is perhaps ironic that dissatisfaction with the performance of teachers has tended to grow as education has become more systematized, yet the "solution" to the perceived decline in literacy and teacher effectiveness has continued to be the increase of program control at the expense of teacher autonony.

Teachers are an endangered species. While being given less and less freedom to teach, they are being held more and more accountable. And in the comparison with technology, teachers are being put at a crucial disadvantage. Teachers are not evaluated on whether children enjoy reading and writing, on how often and extensively children independently engage in reading and writing in their everyday lives, nor even on how fast they learn when the learning is relevant to their own individual interests. Instead children and teachers are evaluated on what the programs teach best, on standardized, decontextualized, fragmented "skills." The majority of reading tests favor programs, because they are restricted to measuring the same kinds of things that programs teach best, isolated facts and skills that can be dealt with one standardized step at a time.

The problem is also that while programs make teachers look ineffectual, teachers (and children) make programs look good. A teacher tells a child to spend an hour on worksheets and at the end of the day there will be time for independent reading. At the end of the year, the child can read and the teacher gives all the credit to the worksheets. The way most teachers are trained not only leads them to be dependent upon programs but to give programs the credit for success, though not the blame for failure.

The Martian Test

Imagine a Martian space traveler sent to earth to investigate the nature and utility of the reading and writing that earthlings find so important. Suppose the Martian decided that classrooms would be the best places to gather information. What would the Martian conclude reading and writing to be from the materials available and from the activities of teachers and children under the influence of programs? Could a reasonable report be sent back to Mars? As I said earlier, the problem may not be that children do not learn in school but that they learn all the time. And, like the Martian, they will learn exactly what is demonstrated. Should we expect children to be any less misled than the Martian?

Conclusions

The critical issue confronting education today is not which programs are best for teaching children to read and to write, but what children will learn. Teachers can teach that literacy is useful, enjoyable, and attainable, provided they are left free to teach in an unprogrammed manner. Programs will teach something else—that literacy is what programs demonstrate.

I am not arguing against technology. I think microprocessors and every other aspect of contemporary technology should be important tools for learning—like typewriters and calculators—but not control devices for teaching. Children should learn to use technology but not to be used by it. The question again is, "Who is in charge?"

Many people can think of teachers who override programs and who engage children in productive language learning. Many teachers believe they themselves are exceptions. And, of course, such teachers exist. My concern is that they may be losing the possibility of teaching. Programs are being thrust upon them, not only by school and political administrations but by parents and the media, all seemingly convinced that programmed education is a universal panacea. It will not help if teachers also believe that programs can only be benign.

Teachers as well as literacy are threatened, and only teachers can resist the threat. They can resist by asserting their crucial role in teaching literacy against all who assert otherwise. In the present decade, the most important educational function of teachers may well be outside the classroom rather than within it.

13
A Metaphor for Literacy—Creating Worlds or Shunting Information?

Metaphors are the legs of language, on which thought steadily advances or makes its more daring leaps. Without metaphor thought is inert, and with the wrong metaphor, it is hobbled. Metaphors are inescapable. Language cannot address reality directly (whatever "reality" might be without metaphor). Metaphors are the analogies by which one thing is explored or discussed in terms of another, the familiar used as a fulcrum to reveal the unknown.

Thought can be entirely contained within metaphorical frameworks that define present and future understanding in an entire realm of inquiry, just as a map summarizes but also constrains travel throughout a geographic region. Such metaphorical structures are known as *models* (or by the more elegant synonym *paradigms*). Models and paradigms are more than perspectives; they are all-encompassing all-confining nets within which thought is organized and trammeled. Thus, metaphor can limit what inquiry will consider.

My argument is that a change of metaphor is required for thinking about language. I shall propose that our perceptions of literacy are narrowed if not distorted by the pervasive tendency, in education as well as in language theory and research, to regard language solely as the means by which information is shunted from one person to another. The model from which I want to escape perceives language as synonymous with communication and communication as the transmission of information, the exchanging of messages like sums of money or bags of oranges. What you get is what you are given. It all seems to me wholly inappropriate and misleading.

It is not only with respect to language that I am concerned with the intellectual fallout from a mushrooming of the information metaphor. Science generally tends to derive its metaphors from contemporary technology. The world, society, individuals,

This paper also appears in David R. Olson, Nancy Torrance, and Angela Hildyard (Eds.), *Literacy, Language and Learning: The Nature and Consequences of Reading and Writing.* (In preparation.)

and especially brains and bodies are widely perceived in terms of computers, as systems that feed off information. The current paradigm in cognitive psychology regards the brain as a repository of information, thought as "information-processing," and learning as the mechanism by which new information is acquired.

I propose to argue that:

1. Very little of what the brain contains can be appropriately thought of as information.
2. Very little of the brain's commerce with the world (including other people) can be appropriately regarded as the exchange of information.
3. Learning is rarely a matter of acquiring information.
4. The brain is not very good at acquiring information; it is not the most "natural" thing for the brain to do.
5. Language is not a particularly efficient means of transmitting information; it is not the most "natural" thing for language to do.

I shall also propose two paradoxes: (1) writing is less efficient than speech for the communication of information, but (2) on the other hand, writing is more "natural" than speech in some important respects; it is better suited to do those things that the brain is more likely to do and is more effective in doing them. Finally, I shall argue that the view in education that the function of writing is the communication of information must have suppressed many potential authors from an early age and also must have done a good deal to lower standards of spelling, punctuation, and other important aspects of the secretary's craft. In other words, the information-transmission metaphor has worked directly against the interests of literacy.

The Alternative

At this point I should perhaps, give some indication of what I am for, a flavor of the metaphor I favor, which I would like to substitute for information-shunting as a way of thinking about language and the brain.

My alternative is that the primary, fundamental, and continual activity of the brain is nothing less than the creation of worlds. *Thought* in its broadest sense is the construction of worlds, both "real" and imaginary, *learning* is their elaboration and modification, and *language*—especially written language—is a particularly "real" and imaginary, *learning* is their elaboration and modification, and *language*—especially written language—is a particularly efficacious but by no means unique medium by which these worlds can be manifested, manipulated, and sometimes shared. My metaphor pictures the brain as an artist, as a creator of experience for itself and for others, rather than as a dealer in information.

It would not be difficult to elaborate upon my metaphor in various ways—to begin to dissect the internally consistent (and sometimes externally validated) systems of knowledge, belief, and possibility that the brain creates, explores, and occasionally communicates. The argument is basically constructivist, not in itself provocative or unusual in other areas of psychology or philosophy, especially with respect to perception and memory. I could analyze the imperatives of this creative process, looking more specifically at the way in which it organizes worlds—including the world we call the "real" one—in terms of imposed categories, attributes of categories, and category interrelationships (Smith, 1975). The metaphor itself could be examined more deeply, looking, for example, at how the term *create* literally means "to cause to come into existence, to generate possibilities of experience." I could enlarge upon the doubly productive nature of creativeness in both art and cognition, first in the generation and selection of alternatives out of which an imaginative product or artifact can be shaped, and then as the artifact itself becomes a source of exploration and discovery for oneself and others, a new source of possibilities in the world, a new world.

But instead I want to put my metaphor to the test, to examine through use my contentions that the creation of worlds is a more productive and appropriate metaphor for language, literacy, and learning than the shunting of information.

Very Little of What the Brain Contains Is Information

Like most of the common and useful words of every language, the word *information* is ambiguous, gaining or losing specific meaning from the context in which it occurs. And like such words as *language, meaning, word,* and *communication,* it can be used very loosely indeed. For example, one can call everything found in a brain, or in a book, "information." But such indiscriminate usage says nothing, because it homogenizes the contents of the brain and leaves us to find another term for those aspects that are indeed informative (just as the assertion that life is but a dream leaves us to find a new term to distinguish the events within our lives that *are* dreams). The brain contains many aspects, affective and conative, feelings and values and intentions, that cannot be called "information" in any meaningful sense.

More specific definitions of information share the characteristic of facilitating decision-making; information is what helps us make up our minds (and is, therefore, something different from "the mind"). The notion that information facilitates decision-making by reducing uncertainty is one of the original and fundamental insights of information theory (Shannon and Weaver, 1949). Information is regarded as any kind of signal, any distinctive feature or significant difference, that reduces uncertainty by eliminating alternative choices. Thus, traffic lights are informative, the red or the green light reducing uncertainty about whether to proceed through an intersection. Information is a difference that makes a difference (Bateson, 1979). Such a notion is inherent in distinctive feature theories of speech production and recognition (Jakobson and Halle, 1956; Miller and Nicely, 1955), and also of reading (Gibson, 1965; Smith and Holmes, 1971). In such a sense, anything in the world can be informative, since anything can be a signal—provided, of course, that it is properly interpreted. Signals that cannot be interpreted, that do not reduce uncertainty, are technically regarded as "noise." In such a sense, information can only exist in the world, not in the brain. What the brain must contain is the understanding that can interpret signals, that can transform noise into information.

A second, more general meaning of the term *information* is "facts," or representations of selected aspects of reality, which may exist in both the world and the brain. Facts come in a variety of forms, in formulae, in maps and diagrams, and in language. It is a fact that Paris is the capital of France, that $2 \times 2 = 4$, that water is wet, and that h-o-r-s-e is the spelling of the word *horse*, which is the name of a particular kind of animal. Facts exist objectively in what Popper (1972) calls "World 3," the world of human artifacts and ideas. And facts exist in the human brain when they have been memorized. Many people, beginning with Samuel Johnson, seem to believe that education is a matter of learning all the facts that one needs to know or learning where to find them. However, like the more specific form of information, facts reduce uncertainty only to the extent that they can be interpreted, even when they have been committed to memory.

A fact in the brain may be more accessible than a fact in a book, but it is still not informative in itself; it still has to be interpreted. That Paris is the capital of France is a fact that is meaningful to me. I also know that Gaborone is the capital of Botswana, but this is less informative to me because I know little else about the city or the country. And the fact that $E = mc^2$ reduces no uncertainty for me at all because I have no idea of how to make use of it, even though I have succeeded in committing it to memory.

In other words, the information that we have in the brain in the form of memorized facts must (like the facts and signals also available in the world around us) be interpreted by something else in the brain, something that is not information but which enables us to make sense of information, which in itself must be far more extensive than the information in the world or in the brain. What is it that we have in the brain that enables us to make sense of the world, to interpret signals and make sense of information? The brain contains nothing less than a *theory of the world* (Smith, 1975), a theory that is an interpreted summary of all past experience—"a history of all the problems an individual has had to solve" (Popper, 1972)—that is the basis not only of our present understanding of the world but more importantly of our predictions of the future.

Such a theory contains all our knowledge, beliefs, and expectations about the objective world in which we find ourselves. We are confused whenever we encounter an occurrence in the world that we cannot relate to our theory and surprised when something occurs contrary to our expectations. Information may have gone into the construction of the theory, but it was constructed of far more than information. The theory was constructed of hypotheses, confirmed or disconfirmed partly on the basis of our experiences of the world around us, partly on the basis of our own internal tests, our thinking. Where did the hypotheses come from? From the theory itself. Nothing the theory cannot hypothesize can be part of the theory (nothing the theory cannot make sense of can be made sense of). What were the theory's original hypotheses? The learning possibilities which we were born with.

To catalog the theory of the world that we have in the head would be to describe the world as we know it, with all its complexities and interrelationships, an impossible Kantian task. A catalog of the theory that we are born with, the innate possibilities of real and imagined worlds, is only just beginning to be studied by developmental psychologists and psycholinguists. Cognitive psychologists are, I think, referring to aspects of the theory of the world when they talk of the *schemas* of memory (Bartlett, 1932) or of thought (Kintsch, 1974, 1977), of *scenarios* (Schank and Abelson, 1977), *plans* (Miller, Galanter, and Pribram, 1960), or *descriptions* (Norman and Bobrow, 1979). All of these are the possibilities that enable us to interact with the world, to make sense of its circumstances and to fulfill our own intentions. When our theory of the world fails, when we cannot use it to interpret what is happening to us, we are like a person stumbling through a dark and unfamiliar room, furnishing it with only what the imagination can bring.

Yet there is much more to the theory that we have in the head than all our understanding of what the world is like. We constantly manipulate the theory—or rather the theory constantly manipulates itself—to explore and experience what the world might be like, what we wish (or are afraid) it could be like or had been like. We construct worlds that would never exist otherwise, in every art form, in language, and in our own heads.

The world in the head is dynamic, constantly changing, both in the course of its own enterprises and in its interactions with the world around. The objective world itself is rarely static. That cars and buses exist may be a relatively permanent part of my theory of the world, but their particular points of existence as I drive along the road is something my theory must continually predict, modify, and erase.

Anticipation leads all our interactions with the world, which is another way of saying that imagination structures reality. Fantasy is not reality manipulated; reality is a fantasy constrained by the objective world. As David Olson has remarked to me, reality is fantasy that works.

The brain is not a repository of information like a library or the memory banks of a computer. Estes (1980) is only the most recent experimental cognitive psychologist to remark that the brain does not store anything at all; it is an interactive organ with a life of its own, constantly changing its state on the basis of its own operations as well as of "information" from the world around. The perceived world is a vast and dynamic canvas which the brain creates, explores, and changes according to its own critieria of logic, intention, and aesthetic preference, with only the minimum necessary regard to the demands of reality, just as a painter will check if a picture is congruent with a particular landscape but will still give priority to the artistic intent.

Very Little of the Brain's Commerce with the World Is the Exchange of Information

Reading is frequently defined as "the acquisition of information from print," and reading is frequently taught and tested as if information-shunting were its sole purpose. Rosenblatt (1980) satirizes the educational perspective in an article entitled "What Facts Does This Poem Teach You?" She distinguishes two pur-

poses for reading—*efferent*, when the object is to acquire information, and *aesthetic*, when the intention is fulfilled within the act
of reading itself. Her complaint is that schools transform what
should be aesthetic reading, performed for the sheer pleasure
and satisfaction of doing it, into the drab and disenchanting
routine of assimilating and regurgitating information.

It is easy to distinguish Rosenblatt's two functions of reading.
Efferent reading is occurring when we would just as soon not be
reading at all—for example, when someone else could tell us the
sports scores, consult the catalog, review the small advertisements, or summarize the day's news. We are rarely held in thrall
by the huge cast of characters, each uniquely identified, in the
telephone directory. With aesthetic reading, on the other hand,
we are reluctant to have the experience end. We are not reading
to acquire information but to explore a world of sensations or
ideas. What we bring to the text is as important as the text itself.
We are annoyed if someone tries to deprive us of the reading by
telling us how the story ends. We slow as we reach the concluding pages of the book in order to extend the experience.

Extending the experience is the basis of most normal discussions (as opposed to the stilted classroom travesties) about books,
movies, plays, television programs, works of art, and events in
everyday life. These are not exchanges of information; no one
may say anything that is not known already, but each helps in the
reconstruction and continuation of aspects of the original experience. Conversations are frequently the same. The participants do
not exchange messages; they weave a fabric, woof and weft,
sometimes creating a tapestry of shared ideas that is indeed a
work of art. A conversation can be like a walk through the woods,
an unmapped meander with no goal beyond the activity itself,
certainly not undertaken for the purpose of coming out on the
other side. The only thing predictable about the ground to be
covered is that the participants will stay within arm's reach of
each other.

Conversations, walks, car journeys, or entire days can be
undertaken for the sake of the experience itself rather than for
reaching a particular destination or achieving a particular end, a
creative rather than a passive enterprise. Even when new "facts"
about the world are assimilated, they become part of the theory of
the world because the theory has reached out and selected them;
they become part of the constructive endeavor. The human brain
is not a vacuum cleaner, mindlessly sucking up every particle of
information in its way. The information routinely gathered by the
brain may often be acquired without awareness or effort, a by-

product of the experience in which we are engaged, but it is always relevant to what is known already.

Much of the time, the world with which we interact is the world in the head, even when we are ostensibly interacting with the world around us. We reflect upon what might be going on, upon what might have been going on, and upon what might be going to go on. The brain does not remain supinely content to take and interpret life as it comes; it creates its experiences. All this is related to aspects of human mental life which I feel have never been satisfactorily explained, such as the apparently universal fascination with panoramas and diaramas, with models and miniatures and scenes from great heights, with intricate constructions and subtle mechanisms. Curiosity and exploration are not explained by being called "drives." Play is essentially creative behavior; it has no apparent purpose beyond the activity itself, and Sutton-Smith (1979) has noted that children's language in play is richer than their language in more mundane activities. Perhaps dreams are the purest instances of the brain constructing worlds, of experience without information.

The brain has difficulty in distinguishing "reality" from fantasy, and not only in children. The "willing suspension of disbelief" that is supposed to constitute the theatrical experience seems to me to have the matter backward; it is belief that is difficult to suspend. A film, or even a book, can move us irresistably to tears, laughter, or fear, no matter how hard we try to tell ourselves "it isn't real." Can we always distinguish what actually happened, what we have read, and what we only imagined in the past? Is reality a fantasy with a tag attached, a tag that can easily be detached?

Learning Is Rarely A Matter of Acquiring Information

We learn without knowing what we learn. A moment's reflection and we can recall—we can construct—what we were wearing yesterday and the day before, details of the meals we had, the people with whom we talked, the newspapers we read, the television programs that we watched. If we cannot remember the specific days, newspapers, or television programs before that, it is not because they have been forgotten but because what we have learned from them has been integrated more generally into our theory of the world; they have become part of everything that we know. Our memory for certain kinds of events of the past is truly remarkable; we recognize faces, spoken and written words, and late-night movies that we have not encountered for years, and the recognition brings with it a broader tissue of recollections.

We learn so easily that learning of the kind I have just illustrated is often not considered to be learning at all, or its pervasiveness is overlooked. This is because the relative difficulty of learning in the structured, deliberate, information-gathering manner of school and formal study is often so conspicuous. The learning that is easy and continual is the learning that is accomplished as part of the daily interaction between the world and the world in our head. It is not the cramming of new information but the elaboration and modification of the theory of the world in the head. "Facts" are often learned consciously, but understanding grows inconspicuously with the development of the theory in the head, in the extension of experience, just as the muscles develop inconspicuously in the practice of an athletic activity.

Learning and experience are inseparable, however the experience occurs. Psychologists have argued that our memory for an event is the way in which we made sense of the event (Tulving and Thomson, 1973), just as Popper (1972) asserted that any individual's knowledge was a history of the problems that the individual had had to solve. The word *experience* comes from the same root as *experiment*: it is more than something that happens; it is a test. The brain learns the way an artist learns, not by accumulating facts but by exploring possibilities, by testing its own creations.

The Brain Is Not Very Good at Acquiring Information

As I have just indicated, learning is often unfairly characterized as a difficult and arduous activity because of the conspicuous effort that it so often seems to entail in an educational context. The brain is a highly efficient learning device, but only when it is actively making sense of something, not when it is consciously striving to assimilate facts. Rote learning, the deliberate effort to memorize unrelated items of information, is so difficult and inefficient as to be clearly unnatural, the brain's least preferred way of learning.

Consider the 100-year history of the "scientific" study of verbal learning in experimental psychology, beginning with the invention of the nonsense syllable by Ebbinghaus (Boring, 1957). Nonsense was required because experimental results were "lawful" and able to be replicated only when subjects could make no sense of the stimuli, when everyone had an equivalent task of striving to memorize by rote a sequence of unrelated facts. Because sense destroys experiments, the history has been one of constant struggle between experimenters trying to contrive better and better nonsense and subjects trying to make sense of it. The only predictable thing about learning when individuals manage to make it meaningful in some way is that it takes place very much quicker than nonsense-learning and lasts a good deal longer. The brain learns best when it is most creative.

The acquisition of information by rote might not in itself be unnatural, since the brain does seem capable of accomplishing it to some degree. But such an effort is so inefficient that any tendency in psychology and in education to regard learning primarily as a matter of difficulty and deliberate intention rather than something more meaningful and creative would appear to be most unnatural indeed.

Language Is Not a Particularly Efficient Means of Communicating Information

The relative inadequacy of language in affective matters is widely recognized, in poetry, in science, and in everyday life. No flood of words can take the place of a look, a sigh, or a touch of the hand in communicating friendship or sympathy. The more subtle the intent, the more impotent language seems to be to express it.

For more general information, however, language is widely regarded not just as an effective medium but often as the exclusive one. In a few summary pages, Popper (1976) pithily disposes of this view. He argues that increased precision can only be achieved in language at the cost of clarity (p. 24); that speakers and writers can never protect themselves completely from being misunderstood (p. 30), because they can never anticipate every context in which their remarks might be interpreted; and that, in fact, we never really know what we are talking about (p. 27), because we can never understand all of the implications of what we say.

There are two fundamental and related problems for language with respect to information transmission, both connected to its strength from other points of view. The first lies in its ambiguity; words and sentences can be interpreted in a variety of ways, not idiosyncratically but with respect to context. The imperative "fire" means one thing at a conflagration and another at an execution. The commonest English nouns can also be verbs or adjectives, or both, often with a variety of senses for each syntactic function. Normally we are not aware of this inherent ambiguity, but only because listeners and readers are able to bring sense to utterances through context, not only the linguistic context but also their own prior knowledge and their understanding of the utterer's specific intentions. The second problem is that the surface structures of language do not represent meaning directly, but rather require interpretation based on the syntactic and semantic intuitions of the recipient.

More precise languages do exist—the languages of logic and mathematics, for example, of knitting patterns and computer programs. Such languages are not as rich and productive as natural language; their applications are limited to the specific contexts in which they occur. What they gain in precision they lose in power. But in any case, such languages do not reflect the way the brain works. None of the world's 3000 or more natural languages functions in the unambiguous information-shunting modes of computers, and all seem much easier to learn (since infants universally have very little difficulty with them).

Natural languages are productive and creative systems, flourishing on inventiveness and initiative in interpretation. What they achieve is limited or extended by what the people who share them can mutually bring to their language exchanges. Language creates a whole new realm of possible experiences for human beings, but it does this by reflecting more the personal characteristics of the individuals who use it on any particular occasion than the "information" that passes between them.

There are more efficient ways of communicating information—in formulae, diagrams, and photographs. It is perhaps significant that none of these media is one in which creative artists typically work, in contrast to natural language, painting, and music, unless the artists go beyond the literal bounds of the medium to impose their own personal vision. It would be foolish to argue that language cannot be used for the transmission of information, but it is far from the sole function of language, and it is not one for which language is particularly suited. That is why we have traffic lights and road maps.

Speech Is Better than Writing for Communication

The question is essentially one of resources. Since language is basically fallible as a means of information transmission, it needs to draw on everything it can to achieve communication effectively. In particular, every possibility must be exploited to capitalize upon the contribution that the recipient must make to understand messages. And language that is spoken has more resources than language that is written.

There is one advantage that every speaker has over writers,

the possibility of using intonation for subtlety and for emphasis. Punctuation, italicizing, capitalizing, and underlining offer only a shadow of the modulating powers of the human voice. And in face-to-face situations the speaker's repertoire is enlarged enormously, not only because a wide range of conventional facial and other physical gestures exists, but also because the speaker can respond from moment to moment to the listener's understanding and uncertainty. When speech can be seen carrying the listener like a surfer upon a wave, the speaker can accelerate, abbreviate, whisper, even become careless without going beyond what the listener will tolerate. When difficulties occur, the speaker can revise, repeat, recall, foreshadow, reemphasize, elaborate, illustrate, and summarize, all in tune with the needs of the listener. None of these resources is available to the writer, deprived of the principal source of the speaker's strength, a close interaction with the recipient. A great deal of communication can take place in the absence of words, in the absence of a common language even, when the two participants can see each other; speech serves to cement shared understandings. But writers and readers must usually interact without appeal to each other's sensitivity (personal letters excepted). They are kept apart by a text which is supposed to unite them but which, like a two-sided mirror, can only reflect back upon them their own images.

Writing is widely supposed to be better than speech for communication, because it is relatively durable and easily transportable. In addition, writing can often be scrutinized at the recipient's pleasure. Entire passages can be reread or skipped. Readers can proceed at their own pace, can move ahead as well as back, without concern for the speed or sequence in which the text was produced. But these aspects of written language do little to enhance communication. If anything, they serve only to dissipate understanding. A text, like any work of art or artifice, serves primarily as a vehicle by which the perceiver's own world constructions, rather than the producer's, are promoted.

Writing is not good for communicating information; it is good only for codifying it. Print freezes language and carries it to new contexts beyond the reach or understanding of the producer, who has no control over how the text will be interpreted. It is truly the language of the blind. This is why texts are always subject to exegesis, why there is interminable haggling over the meaning of testaments, constitutions, laws, contracts, even newspaper articles.

Olson (1977) argues that a strength of written language is that it has to mean what it says. In my view, the great weakness of written language is that it can never be sure of saying what is meant. Writers are always tempted to think that their text is transparent, because they are the ones who know what they wanted to say. They are not only denied the recipient's perspective; they also lose control of the text the moment it is read by someone else. The previously cited quotations from Popper (p. 126) about the limitations of language for anyone who hopes to communicate apply particularly to writing. Written language invites contention and then, by its persistence through time and space, offers every facility for the contention to expand and persist.

Writing Is Better than Speech for the Creation of Worlds

Writing may not be superior to speech for the communication of information, (which, I have argued, neither speech nor the brain itself are very good at in any case), but writing is infinitely more efficacious than speech in another respect: it is superbly more potent in creating worlds. And since I also argue that creating worlds is the brain's primary concern, then I am forced to the conclusion that writing might in some ways be considered more natural than speech; it does better what the brain does best.

Writing is typically regarded as more permanent than speech, for the superficial reason that its manifest form endures longer. But writing is malleable; it is a plastic art. In writing, not only can we create worlds, but also we can change them at will. Writing enables us to explore and change the worlds of ideas and experience that the brain creates. As I argued in Chapter 10, this is the enormous power and attraction of writing, especially for children—until something happens to persuade them that writing does not have this power at all.

The power of writing is not initially lost upon many children. A child who writes "The dog died" is astounded at what has been accomplished. The child has put a dog into the world that did not exist before—created a world that would not otherwise have existed—and then has killed the dog. None of this can be done in any other way. And if the child is contrite, a stroke of the pen is all that is required to bring the dog to life, something else that would be difficult to accomplish in any other way.

It may be argued that the child who has killed the dog will be anxious to show this drama to other people, thus demonstrating a desire to communicate information. Children also like to share what they enjoy reading. But children do not generally have a passion for conveying information to adults (as opposed to making a good impression on them or manipulating their behavior).

Children do not normally expect to be in possession of information that adults do not already have and are likely to be interested in. There are two reasons why children might enjoy having an adult read their first brief literary productions: one is to share the wonder of the creation itself and the second is to show how clever they are. Such motivations are not absent from more adult texts one sometimes finds published in professional journals or pinned on staff room notice boards.

I can anticipate at least two objections to my suggestion that writing might be considered more natural than speech in some important ways. Whereas spoken language is universal, cultures still exist that do not have writing, which appears to be a relatively recent arrival on the human scene. And whereas just about every child can learn to speak at an early age and at a rapid rate in the absence of any formal instruction, writing generally has to be taught, often with considerable difficulty and limited success. My response to the two objections is the same, that writing requires an external technology. *Language* appears to be part of the inherited potential of every child, and in the case of speech it is fortunate that just about every child is also born with a vocal apparatus capable of expressing this potential in audible form. The problem with language from a visual point of view is that it requires tools. When supplied with a convenient instrument, like an electric typewriter, children can learn to write at the age of 2 (Doman, 1975), and there is an extensive literature on children who have learned to read at the age of 2 to 3. To assert that writing is unnatural because it does not occur in many cultures is like arguing that swimming is unnatural because it may not be often or easily learned by people who do not have access to water, like desert dwellers. One does not become a writer if the tools do not lie conveniently at hand, so to speak.

The difficulty that many children encounter in learning to write may also be inseparable from the instruction they receive, a topic to which I shall return in due course when we renew acquaintance with our young dramatist and the saga of the dog that died.

The principal disadvantage of speech is that we usually have very little time to organize it and scarcely any chance at all to reflect upon it or to accommodate intrusive thoughts, either as speakers or listeners. Therefore, it is not well suited for the kind of creative activity that the brain performs best. It may indeed be only because of its relative utility for communication, in conjunction with the other expressive resources that human beings have available, and also because a suitable audible language-production instrument is built in, that speech has persisted as a universal and perhaps somewhat overrated human talent.

Some Practical Implications

My aim is to change a prevailing metaphor. I am not against "communication," nor would I deny its importance or even argue that one should not learn to use language as best one can to accomplish communicative ends. But I feel that both the limitations of language as a medium of communication and the limitations of communication as a metaphor for language should be recognized.

This is not simply a matter of playing with words. As I said at the beginning, the metaphors we choose structure the way we perceive the world. In cognitive psychology, for example, I fear that the tendency to perceive the brain primarily as an information-processing device ignores the most central and most interesting aspects of learning and thought, just as the earlier associative model in the study of verbal learning led to a distorted perception of the nature of memory. Indeed, some of the more extreme applications of an information-processing approach seem to me to have been a reversion to a rigid stimulus-response psychology (for example, Anderson and Bower, 1973), in which comprehension is regarded simply as an ability to respond with a sentence identical to the stimulus. Computer simulations of "language processing" have evaluated models of human understanding in terms of how well they could be translated into computer programs. More recently, schema theories have tended to look at language comprehension in terms of the prior knowledge and expectations of the individual (e.g., Rumelhart, 1975), still often characterized as the "receiver," however. Psychologists are still a long way from studying how individuals construct their personal models of the world, the genesis of their knowledge and expectations.

Something that mildly surprises me is the general drabness of the metaphors that psychology does employ, the unimaginativeness of the theories to which it is inclined. The physicalist model of billiard ball causality, which, to many psychologists, has always seemed the epitome of scientific control and aspiration, is many years out of date, abandoned by physicists themselves. To find exciting and imaginative theories today, throbbing with color and with marvel, one has to turn to astronomy, nuclear physics, or genetic biology. To try to comprehend what is dimly perceived through powerful electron microscopes and telescopes seems to require the mind of a poet. Why, then, should that most remarkable universe of all, the human brain, be approached in such a grey and mechanistic way? Particularly regrettable is the drab and mechanical approach that the communication metaphor often introduces into classrooms. Paradoxically, the desire to produce effective communicators may actually help to destroy the ability of many children to write. The danger is that the information-transmission emphasis can lead to an almost exclusive perception of writing from the perspective of a reader rather than from the writer's point of view.

Let me return to the young author of "The dog died." When this story is read by a teacher who adopts a reader's point of view (and parents also are very good at this), the child will be told something like "It isn't very long, is it? Can't you tell me the dog's name or what color it is?"—as if these facts fall into the same existential category as the birth and death of a living creature in three short words, as if it is the length of a piece of writing that matters. Worse, an adult's comment might have something to do with two spelling mistakes and a punctuation error in those three short words, scarcely likely to encourage the child to write longer fragments in the future and certainly not with words of which the spelling is in doubt.

The consequence of premature and exclusive concern with the reader's point of view is that schools attempt to produce secretaries instead of authors. Children are expected to learn to spell and punctuate as their admission fee to the privilege of writing, and such a procedure not only inhibits potential authors, denying to many children both the pleasure and the learning opportunities of spontaneous personal writing, but it produces awful secretaries as well. I am not arguing that spelling and punctuation are not important but that instruction which gets in the way of a child's writing will just not succeed in its aims. A consequence of such failures, reinforced by the general perceptions that literacy is both difficult and solely for communication, is that reading and writing are fatally trivialized. Children may not be exposed to reading as a compelling aesthetic experience. They may not have writing demonstrated to them as a means of creating worlds which they themselves can experience and explore (and which they may, if they wish, subsequently decide to share with others). They may be subjected to drills and homilies that teach them that literacy is work, punitive, and a bore. Even if they do "learn to write," what they will learn is that the purpose of reading and writing is the shunting of information.

Such is the lesson that seems well learned by many college

students. They are reasonably good at writing if they are told what exactly to write, and when, and how much. They are very competent in quoting the views of others (with the references beautifully displayed) and even in providing summary statements. But they are most unconvincing in constructing their own point of view or in arguing for or against the views of others, because they have rarely had the experience of doing so.

Concluding Constructions

I am not proposing a solipsistic point of view. I am not arguing that the brain as an artist actually creates the objective, physical world which the body as a whole inhabits. World-creating is not an asocial activity; the brain's theory is constrained by its shareability (at least in those aspects of the theory that must be shared with other people). The closeness of two individuals' theories of the world doubtless reflects the closeness of their cultures and of their roles and stations in those cultures. The world that the brain creates is at the same time personal, social, and physical. Readers of the same book can share the same experience, to the extent that two people can ever share the same experience. Indeed, written language permits very special kinds of experience to be shared, from myth to science, from narrative to poetry.

I also do not wish to communicate or create pessimism and despair. The shelves of our libraries may buckle under compendiums of information, but they can also be replete with good stories, insightful observations, and interesting ideas. I hear of many individuals, in educational institutions and out, who have difficulty in coping with all the information to which they are exposed (let alone that which they do not understand), but I rarely hear anyone complain of the wealth of reward and pleasure that written language so prodigiously provides, the possibilities of a broader experience of the world around and of the public and private worlds that we ourselves construct.

Finally, I do not want to suggest that my proposed change of metaphor will be easy. A considerable difficulty with perceiving the brain as an artist is that it does not facilitate control or "accountability" in educational contexts or replication in psychological experiments. Creativeness is not easily quantified. The contents of the human brain are so vast that sheer description is out of the question. If the value of a model is determined by the rigor with which it can be evaluated, then the brain as artist looks like getting as short shrift as any struggling artist in these days of "objective" economic decisions. The relative value of metaphors cannot be assessed "objectively." There is no statistical test that will decide which is "correct." The question is which metaphor is the most productive, and the answer will depend on what one's intention is in the first place—to measure and control human behavior or to understand it.

Afterthoughts

Most of the papers in this volume began life as parts of unscripted talks and workshop discussions, subject to questions, comments, interruptions, and arguments. If there had been no questions and comments, there would almost certainly have been no papers, because I rarely set ideas in print without first seeing how they fare with other people. Ideas are like children; they are shaped and flourish best in social situations.

Some questions arise so frequently at the conclusion of my public addresses that they have become old friends; I look for them in the audience and miss them if they fail to make an appearance. They provide me with opportunities to underline points that I seem unable to make adequately in the formal part of presentations, to try to make myself clear, or to say what I should have said earlier.

With published papers, one must usually be content with just one chance, meeting silence with silence as one's words lie cold and still on the snowfields of the printed page. But with a collection like the present volume, as I look back, it is not difficult to hear echoes of familiar questions and to take advantage of the possibility of responding to them.

Q. *Do you ever have second thoughts?*

A. Frequently. I often change my mind about what I have said but that is surely the basis of learning. It is reckless to claim infallibility, especially in matters as complex as the workings of the human brain and as delicate as the processes of education. Those who presume to "correct" the thinkers of the past should surely realize that they in turn are destined to be revised, by others if not by themselves. I regard my published writing and my talks as explorations of topics that others and I can then think about further. I would hate to be "chained" to what I have said in the past. An example is the use of the information-processing metaphor for understanding language and the brain, which I used extensively in my early writing on reading and which I now argue is both constraining and inappropriate (see Chapter 13). I also think I gave too little attention originally to how much collaboration a child needs in order to learn to read and to write, not in the form of deliberate instruction but as an apprenticeship, working alongside interested others who already know how to do what the child sees some purpose in learning.

I can also have second thoughts about the way I have said something. Occasionally, I feel I have been too restrained, too sensitive to the sensibilities of others. At other times, the reverse is true. The first chapter in this book is a good illustration. This is the paper of mine that has been most extensively republished at other people's request, and it is also the one that embarrasses me most. It is intemperate, harsh, and insistent (even after I have taken the opportunity to edit out some of the blunter assertions).

The "politics" paper (Chapter 1) is an interesting example of what happens to theorists (like Postman and myself) when they are invited to step outside their particular areas of expertise and make general pronouncements about education. At one time, I was extremely critical of academics who leapt incautiously from their narrow base in linguistics, in perceptual or cognitive psychology, in learning theory, to make sweeping statements about the way reading or writing should be taught. I still am critical when I think they do so for reasons of financial gain, or for acclaim, or even as part of a personal campaign to change the world. But I now know that there are occasions, like the one on which Postman and I succumbed, when the theorist is not just invited to step outside a realm of competence and authority but is positively encouraged to do so. Our arms are twisted; we are told that we are evading our responsibilities in declining to take a public stand on some subject or other. We get carried away, which is what I think happened when I tried to grapple with Postman.

Incidentally, I am sometimes asked whether Postman had second thoughts about what he had said as a consequence of reading my paper. He had not; his only published comment was that he did not understand it.

Q. *Why are you so rude about teachers?*

A. I try not to be. I am sorry when I am interpreted in that way. Individual teachers sometimes do remarkably stupid things in classrooms, but usually because that is how they have been trained or because some program, test, or set of objectives binds them to such behavior. Teachers frequently feel they do not have the freedom to make intelligent decisions. But my general argument is that teachers should be trusted. They could be much better than the programs and other constraints allow them to be, and very often they succeed despite the obstacles in their way (and ironically, it is the obstacles, whether other people or programs, that are likely to get the credit for success). I see teachers as victims, not instigators, of reactionary and inhibiting forces in education. My principal criticism of teachers is not that they do not know how to make appropriate decisions but that they are insufficiently active educationally and politically to assert their unique authority to carry these decisions out.

Q. *Isn't it true that what you say about language and learning is impossible in a classroom of thirty children?*

A. Possibly. There is certainly a conflict. But we are talking about two different realities, one very difficult to modify and the other essentially unchangeable. The unchangeable reality is the human brain, which will not alter its nature to suit the contingencies of the classroom. The way children learn is the way children learn, no matter what pressures and constraints are laid upon teachers in classrooms. Schools are a different kind of reality, determined not so much by the nature of children's brains (whatever we might sentimentally like to think) but by the day-to-day exigencies of maintaining the existence and smooth running of bureaucratically organized institutions.

Schools do not reflect the lively, searching, and productive character of children's brains, but the way children's brains function is not a particularly powerful consideration in the organization of schools. I would not be so unrealistic as to suggest that teachers are entirely free to work with children as their own intuitions and formal analyses of language and meaningful learning indicate would be most appropriate. On the other hand, teachers might do more to protect themselves and children from the extreme consequences of the way schools are organized by recognizing that the two realities are in conflict. The programmatic technology of contemporary instruction, straining to "deliver" testable units of information or skill to children on schedule and in forms by which teachers can be held accountable for continuous acquisition, is inevitably antagonistic to the manner in which children necessarily strive to learn. Society may impose all kinds of difficulties and irrelevancies upon what goes on in and around classrooms, but everyone would gain if teachers could recognize these diversions and discuss them openly with their students. Every child understands ritual; every child understands being given an activity in order to be kept quiet. Children are harmed less by nonsense or trivia than by their being persuaded that the nonsense or trivia are important. The least teachers can do is to help children distinguish the wheat from the chaff.

Q. *How can teachers find the time to give children the individual attention required by your ideas of learning?*

A. Recognition of the way children most easily learn to become literate does not entail inordinate amounts of individual attention. Quite the reverse. When groups of children are engaged in long-term collaborative reading and writing activities, working to purposes that they understand and able to help each other or even to seek help outside the classroom, teachers gain time to devote to individual children in productive ways. The most compelling constraints on the time of teachers lie in the individual attention required in handing out, explaining, monitoring, collecting, scoring, recording, and helping children recover from tests and programmatic materials.

Q. *How can you teach a child who isn't interested to read and write?*

A. You can't, won't, and shouldn't try. A child who is bored with reading and writing—or with what passes for reading and writing in the classroom—will only learn that reading and writing are boring. This is a disagreeable but inescapable fact. The task of the reading and writing teacher is not so much to teach those "subjects" as to make literacy interesting and attainable by engaging children in enterprises that have meaning and purpose to them.

Q. *How will children learn if they are not continually corrected, especially on such important matters as spelling and pronunciation?*

A. Children do not learn from being corrected but from wanting to do things the right way. Most of the immense labor teachers put into correcting their students' work is wasted; it is ignored. If it is not ignored, then it may have a negative effect, with children avoiding the words they fear they cannot spell or pronounce correctly. They do not become better spellers or speakers by writing and talking less. Correction is useful, and it is only paid serious attention to, when the student wants it and would indeed be offended if it were not given. Many teachers cannot imagine students wanting to have their spelling mistakes corrected, but the reluctance is a consequence of purposeless activities that must be going on in the classroom, from the students' point of view at least. Children and young people engaged in an activity for a purpose of their own want to do it right. They no more want spelling mistakes in the poster they put on the wall, the story they are circulating, or the letter they will mail than they want to remain ignorant of the fact that they have a speck of mud on their face or some hair sticking up at the back.

Q. *You seem to suggest that children should be encouraged to read and write no matter how many mistakes they make. Don't you have any standards?*

A. The argument is not about standards but about how to achieve them. My feeling about education today is that we settle for too little; our expectations are too low. Most children are capable of much more than they achieve at school. Children themselves should expect to become much more competent readers, writers, spellers, punctuators, and all the rest than they usually turn out to be. The problem is the way in which we expect to attain those standards. If a child attempting to read and write is discouraged because of the emphasis on what is done wrong— "Don't give me any more stories to read if they're going to be full of spelling mistakes"—then the child will simply read and write less. Spelling, punctuation, phonics, and so on are not a set of tools that must be mastered before beginning to read and write. Concentration on the "basics" may be just the experience to turn a child away forever from learning to become literate. In contrast, children who want to practise reading and writing, who see themselves as literate even at the very beginning of learning, are precisely the individuals who demand and achieve high standards.

Q. *Do you really have no room for phonics, or for spelling rules? Surely they are necessary for children who have special difficulties.*

A. I have never argued that the spelling-to-sound correspondences of written and spoken language should be concealed from children, but neither should their complexity and unreliability. Of course, an understanding of these correspondences is a help in the identification of new words, especially if the learner also uses context cues and looks for familiar morphemic elements. But letters and their relationship to sounds do not even begin to make sense to children until they are comfortably familiar with reading meaningful print. It is not that a thorough knowledge of letters is required in order to read words but that a wide acquaintance with words is the only thing that makes sense of letters. No one would try to teach a child her name by saying, "Look, that word is 'Jane', juh - ay - nuh - silent eee." But it would be meaningful and even helpful for Jane, when she can recognize her name and a few others, to be told that her name looks the same as Jean's but different from Ruth's because *J* can be pronounced "juh" and *R* can't.

I suspect that children who learn to read without a significant amount of formal instruction still learn a good deal about spelling-to-sound correspondences. I doubt very much whether they could fail to recognize the consistencies and patterns that occur. Research has not been done on this matter, but that is because it is difficult these days to show that children who have learned to read out of school have not been exposed to some phonics through television, through workbooks for infants that can now be bought in supermarkets, or from oversolicitous parents. However, while it is difficult to show experimentally—though not logically—that children can only make sense of phonics to the extent that they can read, there is absolutely no evidence for the other point of view that facility in phonics makes a reader. Many children, unfortunately, are drilled in phonics for years and still fail to learn to read. Even when they do succeed, it is invalid to claim that it was the phonics instruction that made them into readers, since few children are entirely deprived of access to meaningful print in their lives, if only on street signs, catalogs, and television advertising. But I would not trust the more exuberant educational programmers not to try to deny children even those sources of sense in the future.

As for the notion that immersion in meaningful print might be all very well for bright or "average" children but that surely those who are having difficulties need a more structured approach, my point of view is exactly opposite. Children who are confidently succeeding in becoming literate can tolerate ritual and nonsense; they have an adequate idea of how written language works as a basis for making sense of instruction. But those having difficulty in understanding what is going on are most vulnerable to the distortion of drills and tests and most need the guidance and security of meaningful encounters with written language. Of course, it can be demonstrated that such children learn from drill: they will learn what is drilled into them, but the utility of the "skills" they acquire and the price they may pay in general interest and understanding for acquiring them are issues that the proponents of highly structured instruction rarely consider.

Q. *You seem to talk less these days about ongoing research into the process of reading, into perceptual and cognitive issues, and more about studies of the circumstances in which literacy is learned and attempted to be taught. Does this reflect a change in your own interests?*

A. I follow what I find most illuminating and productive. But I also think there is a greater need at the moment to understand the factors that get in the way of children becoming literate than to expect some great theoretical breakthrough to make a difference in the way children should be taught. From the point of view of reading instruction, I think that sufficient experimental evidence is in. Children learn whatever is demonstrated to them, regardless of what we think or hope they are being taught. Teachers should not expect to have their pedagogical questions answered by cognitive psychological or neurophysiological research, which cannot tell them anything relevant to what should be demonstrated in classrooms. We certainly are not yet in a position to guarantee that every child will learn to read and write, but not because of a lack of understanding about how the brain makes sense of language. The difficulties, as I have tried to show in my most recent articles, are essentially pragmatic and political: They are a question of who is in control in classrooms and of the price we are willing to let children pay for what we feel is the necessary way that they should be taught.

On the matter of the physiology of learning and thought, I am fascinated but not impressed by the recent studies and theories of bilateral brain function and hemispheric specialization. The fact that one side of the brain might be more involved with spatial and affective concerns and the other with sequential and analytical processes tells me nothing about how children should be taught to read and write. All people use all their brains, except for those unfortunate and obvious few who have literally had their cerebral hemispheres bifurcated by natural or surgical trauma. Of course, individuals have preferences about how they learn and what they learn, but that was known long before the studies of hemispheric specialization. Current brain research is once more being used as a rather heavy-handed metaphor, and even as a justification or excuse, for the particular ways we want to teach and to classify children.

I once said that it would not and should not make the slightest difference to the way literacy is taught if it was discovered that a critical neural center for reading was located in the big toe (the left one, naturally, for most people). But even then I would not be surprised to hear some experts diagnosing that certain children had a minimal ingrowing toenail syndrome because they had difficulty with the alphabet.

Q. *Have you ever seen a classroom that meets with your approval? What would your ideal school be like?*

A. I have seen many ideal classrooms at the extremes of the educational range—in kindergartens and in high school. The cause has always been the same, a teacher totally interested not in "instructing" his or her charges but in working alongside them in particular forms of enterprise. Elementary school teachers also exist with such qualities, but their task is harder. There are usually tighter constraints on what they do and on how successfully they must "perform." Elementary school teachers are particularly responsible to the next teacher in line for the specific "progress" of the students they graduate at the end of every year.

Kindergarten teachers often are free to share the wonder of learning with their children; they collaborate with them in their early adventures in art, music, and literature. Teachers and children play together. There is a love and companionship that can be quickly lost in the more structured world of the primary classroom. Oddly, perhaps, the possibility of this collaborative relationship often returns at the secondary level, not in classrooms where a tired and jaded classroom manager endeavors to cram "learning" into uninterested students, but where a subject area specialist—a musician, perhaps, or a cook, carpenter, poet, astronomer, or geologist—first conveys to students a consuming interest in whatever he or she happens to be teaching and then inspires and assists them to do these things themselves. These teachers are not antagonists; they are competent allies to whom students can apprentice themselves.

It is significant that the "master teachers" (of either sex) of whom I talk are not necessarily lax and undemanding with their students. They do not lower standards or minimize effort, nor do they go out of their way to make their subjects "fun." Some of them indeed may be irascible curmudgeons, blocks off the old Mr. Chips, but they have a respect for what they teach and for those who will share their interest. One feels that they would be doing what they are teaching even if they were not teachers.

My ideal school would be very simple. It would have no room for anyone who was not a learner, whether student, teacher, administrator, or visitor, in primary school, the intermediate and secondary grades, and right through university as well. Schools should be learning emporia where people go when they want to engage in the spirit of learning, from which anything that would suppress or inhibit learning would be excluded. I cannot imagine any child not wanting to be part of such a school.

I once told a distinguished professor at a renowned university how much I felt I learned from my students, how I always told them that they had as much to contribute as I had. He was surprised and dismayed. "If you admit to your students that they might know more than you do," he said, "what defense do you have against them?" On the other hand, a woman who had spent many years teaching students of all ages, from kindergarten to university graduates, told me that she would never teach a lesson unless it included something she herself did not know and wanted to find out about. The difference between the two attitudes reflects some of the obstacles standing in the way of my learning emporia and some of the spirit that is thereby excluded from many classrooms.

Q. *What is the best method of teaching reading?*

A. This is often a catch question. I am asked it so that I can be categorized. Sometimes the question is a quick test to find out whether I am on the right side. If I provide a testimonial for the method the questioner already prefers, then I may be worth listening to; otherwise I can be ignored.

But I will not give testimonials for methods, not even for those produced or recommended by the people with whom I generally agree. For a start, most "methods" are subject to wide ranges of interpretation; what one teacher claims to be doing in the name of a particular method may be nothing like what other adherents of the same label subscribe to. And then, even the most sensible of devices and techniques is subject to misuse in the hands of certain teachers. Some teachers could make students anxious handing out free milk. But most important, I do not think methods help children accomplish anything they might usefully want to learn; teachers must do that. Teachers who need to be told the best method would probably not be capable of succeeding with it, even if it existed.

In any case, I do not think a "best method" for teaching children to read and write will ever exist, given the enormous variety in the interests and experience of children and in the circumstances in which they will be best able to make sense of literacy. All that children need is competent people to help them make sense and make use of written language. This is bad news for teachers (and I still encounter them) who believe that "research" will identify the foolproof method of teaching reading. Somebody in reading research must have been doing a good job of public relations. Tens of thousands of research studies have been done, none of which has yet isolated a best method of teaching reading. Why else would so many theorists and educators hold such contradictory points of view? Not one study has been done to demonstrate that such an ideal method could possibly exist.

Q. *Have you ever taught reading yourself?*

A. This also is a frequent question and can be even more of a trap than the last one. My response depends upon what I divine the intention of the questioner to be. If I believe the question is a straightforward request for information, like asking me if I have ever been to the Soviet Union, then I give a straightforward answer: No, I have never taught grade school. Sometimes, however, the question seems to assert that my views about language and the way children learn must be wrong because such contrary things go on in classrooms, and I launch into my discussion of the two largely incompatible realities, school and the brain. If the questioner seems to imply that I am ignorant of some critical considerations, then I might talk about the hundreds of teachers I have worked with and learned from over the years. Sometimes the question is a little more dismissive, a broad suggestion that if I have never taught then I do not know what I am talking about. I may then respond that my wife's obstetrician never had a baby.

But sometimes the question is a genuine request for information about my credentials and my background, in which case I am not reluctant to elaborate. I acknowledge that not only have I never taught classes anywhere outside university, but that I was a late starter even at doing that. Teaching has been my second career. My youthful ambition in England was always to be a writer, and I spent the first 20 years of my working life as a newspaper reporter, magazine writer, editor, and novelist. (An academic acquaintance once claimed that I never stopped writing fiction). I was in my thirties and working on a newspaper in Australia when I first went to college, primarily to engage my curiosity about language in courses on philosophy, literature, anthropology, psychology, and linguistics.

In the 1960s, the excitement of the work of Noam Chomsky, George Miller, and others in the United States in the flourishing new discipline of psycholinguistics had even reached Australia, and at the end of my undergraduate studies I had the opportunity to do doctoral work with Miller at the Center for Cognitive Studies at Harvard. I joined a group of hard-nosed experimentalist cognitive psychologists and did my doctoral dissertation in an area which I would now regard as narrow, technical, and only peripherally related to reading, namely the visual perception of letters of the alphabet.

In those days, when the United States believed that the children's literacy problems could be solved by linguistic experts and program developers in research and development laboratories, a person with a background in psycholinguistics and a dissertation on letter perception was ipso facto an expert in reading. My first two postdoctoral positions were in American educational research centers where I learned everything I have since disagreed with about teaching children to read and to write.

If my studies of the visual system made me an expert in reading, then my status in reading apparently qualified me to become a teacher of teachers, and my first university post required me to give courses of reading to graduate students of education in Toronto. Since I had never taken a course on reading (or even on education), I decided that the last thing I should do was tell teachers how to teach reading. Instead, I discussed with them how I thought reading was accomplished from the child's perspective, and the first book I wrote about reading took the same approach. Remarkably, not only did many teachers understand what I was talking about, but also they felt that my analyses helped to explain why many of the things they were required to do in the classroom did not work as well as the things they did more intuitively or independently. I was providing "scientific" support for many of their own ideas. And my students began to teach me, not just about how children contend with the problems of learning in classrooms, but also about schools and the problems of teachers in general.

Q. *What have you left out of what you have written about literacy?*

A. I cannot list the things I have not thought of, that I am not aware of having overlooked, but I know I have not done enough in several areas that are essential to a complete understanding of literacy.

The first concerns the collaborative manner in which children learn to read and write, a matter in which they are, to extend George Miller's felicitous term for the learning of spoken language, "spontaneous apprentices" (Miller, 1977). Children learn from people they would like to emulate, whether it is a matter of learning to talk, ride bicycles, skate, swim, fish, smoke, swear, or hold up gas stations. In the terms that I started to employ in the paper that is Chapter 11, children engage in learning with someone who does something that they want and expect to do themselves and who will help them to do so. The collaborative nature of the teacher-learner relationship in literacy does not require deliberate instruction or that children should work everything out independently. It is a mutual undertaking, the nature of which has not yet been fully examined by researchers.

This leads to my second underestimated consideration, that literacy is always a cultural phenomenon. What constitutes literacy in one culture is not necessarily the same in another. Children learn to become literate, or to resist literacy, or to fail in it, in sociocultural contexts. And all of this is not simply a matter of whether one's parents are literate or expect literacy, but of the whole social context in which a child is expected to learn or to fail.

I have experienced two quite staggering personal realizations recently. The first was that not all cultures regard literacy as an unalloyed blessing. It may, with good reason, be perceived as a threat to social coherence, personal independence, tradition, and memory. The second realization was that in all cultures literacy can create tensions, among children, teachers, and parents. The two realizations came to me at a symposium at the University of Victoria, Canada, in which psychologists and educators tried to discuss with anthropologists and sociologists the topic of literacy.

I have doubts about how well the participants heard each other, but the papers they presented can be found in a companion volume to this book entitled *Awakening to Literacy*, edited by Goelman, Oberg, and Smith (1983).

The final topic I know I have insufficiently considered is the revolution that microcomputers are beginning to bring about in schools, and thus in literacy. At the moment, I do not even know if their influence will be for the better or the worse, but I do not think anyone else does either. As I tried to explain in Chapter 12, anything microcomputers currently do they do with great power and effect, like bulldozers in rose gardens. They could well destroy the teaching profession and literacy if they are permitted to function as devices for dispensing information and drills. On the other hand, microcomputers might well expand literacy beyond anything we can imagine, in the same way that they are bringing new dimensions to art and to music, provided they are used as tools to help children write and are used primarily by children. Microcomputers must be closely watched.

References

Anderson, John R. and Bower, Gordon H. *Human Associative Memory*. Washington, D.C.: Winston, 1973.

Atkinson, Richard C. Teaching children to read using a computer. *American Psychologist*. 1974, *29*, 169–178.

Atkinson, Richard C. and Shiffrin, Robert M. The control of short-term memory. *Scientific American*, August, 1970, 82–90.

Bartlett, Frederick C. *Remembering*. Cambridge, England: Cambridge University Press, 1932.

Bateson, Gregory. *Mind and Nature*. New York: Macmillan, 1979.

Bettelheim, Bruno. *The Uses of Enchantment: The Meaning and Importance of Fairy Tales*. New York: Knopf, 1976.

Bond, Gerald and Dykstra, Robert. The cooperative research program in first-grade reading. *Reading Research Quarterly*, 1967, **2**, 5–142.

Boring, Edwin G. *A History of Experimental Psychology*. New York: Appleton-Century-Crofts, 1957.

Chafe, Wallace L. *Meaning and the Structure of Language*. Chicago: University of Chicago Press, 1970.

Chall, Jeanne S. *Learning to Read: The Great Debate*. New York: McGraw-Hill, 1967.

Cherry, Colin. *On Human Communication: A Review, a Survey and a Criticism*. 2nd ed. Cambridge, MA: MIT Press, 1966.

Chomsky, Carol. Reading, writing and phonology. *Harvard Educational Review*. 1970, **40**, 287–309.

Chomsky, Noam and Halle, Morris. *The Sound Pattern of English*. New York: Harper & Row, 1968.

Clark, Margaret. *Young Fluent Readers*. London: Heinemann Educational Books, 1976.

Davis, F. B. (Ed.). *The Literature of Research in Reading with Emphasis on Models* (USOE Final Rep.). Washington, DC: U.S. Government Printing Office, 1971. (ERIC Document Reproduction Service No. ED 059 023).

Doman, Glenn. *How to Teach Your Baby to Read*. New York: Doubleday, 1975.

Downing, John and Oliver, Peter. The child's conception of a word. *Reading Research Quarterly*, 1974, **4**, 568–82.

Estes, William K. Is human memory obsolete? *American Scientist*, 1980, **68**, 62–69.

Ferreiro, Emilia. What is written in a written sentence? A developmental answer. *Journal of Education*, 1978, **160**, 25–39.

Fillion, Bryant; Smith, Frank; and Swain, Merrill. Language basics for language teachers: Toward a set of universal considerations. *Language Arts*, 1976, **53**, 740–745, 747.

Fillmore, Charles J. The case for case. In Bach, E. and Harms, R. T. (Eds.), *Universals in Linguistic Theory*. New York: Holt, Rinehart & Winston, 1968.

Fries, Charles C. *American English Grammar*. Appleton-Century, 1940.

Garner, Wendell R. *Uncertainty and Structure as Psychological Concepts*. New York: Wiley, 1962.

Getzels, Jacob W. and Czikszentmihalyi, Mihaly. The creative artist as an explorer. In Hunt, J. McV. (Ed.), *Human Intelligence*. New Brunswick, NJ: Transaction Inc., 1972.

Gibson, Eleanor J. Learning to read. *Science*, 1965, **148**, 1066–1072.

Goodman, Kenneth S. The psycholinguistic nature of the reading process. In Goodman, Kenneth S. (Ed.), *The Psycholinguistic Nature of the Reading Process*. Detroit, Mich.: Wayne State University Press, 1968.

Goodman, Kenneth S. Analysis of oral reading miscues: Applied psycholinguistics. *Reading Research Quarterly*, 1969, **5**, 1, 9–30.

Goodman, Kenneth S. Reading: A psycholinguistic guessing game. In Singer, Harold and Ruddell, Robert (Eds.), *Theoretical Models and Processes of Reading*. Newark, Del.: International Reading Association, 1970.

Goodman, Yetta. The roots of literacy. In Douglass, Malcolm P. (Ed.), *Claremont Reading Conference Forty-Fourth Yearbook*. Claremont, CA, 1980.

Goody, Jack and Watt, Ian. The consequences of literacy. In Goody, Jack (Ed.), *Literacy in Traditional Societies*. Cambridge, England: Cambridge University Press, 1968.

Gough, Philip B. One second of reading. In Kavanagh, James and Mattingly, Ignatius G. (Eds.), *Language by Ear and by Eye: The Relationships Between Speech and Reading*. Cambridge, MA: MIT Press, 1972.

Greenberg, J. H. (Ed.) *Universals of Language*. Cambridge, MA: MIT Press, 1963.

Halliday, Michael A. K. *Explorations in the Functions of Language*. London: Arnold, 1973.

Halliday, Michael A. K. and Hasan, R. *Cohesion in English*. London: Longman, 1976.

Hanna, Paul R.; Hodges, Richard E.; and Hanna, Jean S. *Spelling: Structure and Strategies*. Boston: Houghton-Mifflin, 1971.

Havelock, Eric. *Origins of Western Civilization*. Toronto: Ontario Institute for Studies in Education, 1976.

Hiebert, Elfrieda H. Developmental patterns and interrelationships of preschool children's print awareness. *Reading Research Quarterly*, 1981, **16**, 236–260.

Hochberg, Julian. Components of literacy: Speculations and exploratory research. In Levin, Harry and Williams, Joanna P. (Eds.), *Basic Studies on Reading*. New York: Basic Books, 1970.

House, E. R.; Glass, G. V.; McLean, L. D.; and Walker, D. F. No simple answer: Critique of the follow-through evaluation. *Harvard Educational Review*, 1978, **48**, 128–160.

Huey, Edmund B. *The Psychology and Pedagogy of Reading*. Cambridge, MA: MIT Press, 1968. (Originally published, 1908.)

Jakobson, Roman, and Halle, Morris. *Fundamentals of Language*. The Hague: Mouton, 1956.

Kavanagh, James F., and Mattingly, Ignatius G. (Eds.), *Language by Ear and by Eye: The Relationships Between Speech and Reading*. Cambridge, MA: MIT Press, 1972.

Kintsch, Walter. *The Representation of Meaning in Memory*. Hillsdale, NJ: Erlbaum, 1974.

Kintsch, Walter. On comprehending stories. In Just, Marcel A. and Carpenter, Patricia A. (Eds.), *Cognitive Processes in Comprehension*. Hillsdale, NJ: Erlbaum, 1977.

Kolers, Paul. Three stages of reading. In Levin, Harry and Williams, Joanna P. (Eds.), *Basic Studies on Reading*. New York: Basic Books, 1970.

Liberman, Alvin M. The grammar of speech and language. *Cognitive Psychology*, 1970, **1**, 301–323.

Liberman, Isobel Y., and Shankweiler, David. Speech, the alphabet and teaching to read. In Resnick, Lauren B. and Weaver, Phyllis A. (Eds.), *Theory and Practice of Early Reading* (Vol. 2). Hillsdale, NJ: Erlbaum, 1979.

Lindsay, Peter H. and Norman, Donald A. *Human Information Processing* (2nd. ed.) New York: Academic Press, 1977.

Macnamara, John. Cognitive basis of language learning in infants. *Psychological Review*, 1972, **79**, 1–13.

Mattingly, Ignatius G. Reading, the linguistic process, and linguistic awareness. In Kavanagh, James F. and Mattingly, Ignatius G. (Eds.), *Language by Ear and by Eye*. Cambridge, MA: MIT Press, 1972.

Miller, George A.; Galanter, Eugene; and Pribram, Karl H. *Plans and the Structure of Behavior*. New York: Holt, Rinehart & Winston, 1960.

Miller, George A. and Nicely, Patricia E. An analysis of perceptual confusions among some English consonants, *Journal of the Acoustical Society of America*, 1955, **27**, 338–353.

Murray, Donald M. *A Writer Teaches Writing*. Boston: Houghton Mifflin, 1968.

Neisser, Ulric. *Cognitive Psychology*. New York: Appleton-Century-Crofts, 1967.

Nelson, Katherine. Concept, word and sentence: Interrelations in acquisition and development. *Psychological Review*, 1974, **81**, 267–285.

Norman, Donald A. and Bobrow, Daniel G. Descriptions: An intermediate stage in memory retrieval, *Cognitive Psychology*, 1979, **11**, 107–123.

Olson, David R. From utterance to text: The bias of language in speech and writing, *Harvard Educational Review*, 1977, **3**, 257–281.

Olson, David R., and Bruner, Jerome S. Learning through experience and learning through media. In Olson, David R. (Ed.), *Media and Symbols: The Forms of Expression, Communication and Education*, 73rd Yearbook of the NSSE. Chicago: University of Chicago Press, 1974.

Piaget, Jean. *The Language and Thought of the Child*. London: Routledge and Kegan Paul, 1959.

Popper, Karl. *Objective Knowledge: An Evolutionary Approach*. Oxford, England: Clarendon, 1972.

Popper, Karl. *Unended Quest: An Intellectual Autobiography*. London: Fontana/Collins, 1976.

Postman, Neil. The politics of reading. In Winklejohann, Rosemary (Ed.), *The Politics of Reading*. Newark, Delaware: IRA/ERIC, 1973.

Rosenblatt, Louise M. What facts does this poem teach you? *Language Arts*, 1980, **57**, 4, 384–394.

Rumelhart, David E. Notes on a scheme for stories. In Bobrow, Daniel and Collins, A. (Eds.), *Representation and Understanding: Studies in Cognitive Science*. New York: Academic Press, 1975.

Rumelhart, David E. Toward an interactive model of reading. In Dornic, S. (Ed.), *Attention and Performance VI*. Hillsdale, NJ: Lawrence Erlbaum Associates, 1977.

Samuels, S. Jay. Letter-name versus letter-sound knowledge in learning to read. *The Reading Teacher*, 1971, **24**, 604–608.

Samuels, S. Jay. The effect of letter-name knowledge on learning to read. *American Educational Research Journal*, 1972, **9**, 65–74.

Sartre, Jean Paul. *The Words*. New York: Braziller, 1964.

Schank, Roger C. and Abelson, Robert P. *Scripts, Plans, Goals and Understanding.* Hillsdale, NJ: Erlbaum, 1977.

Shannon, Claude E. Prediction and entropy of printed English. *Bell Systems Technical Journal*, 1951, **30**, 50–64.

Shannon, Claude E. and Weaver, Warren. *The Mathematical Theory of Communication.* Urbana, IL: University of Chicago Press, 1949.

Simon, Herbert. How big is a chunk? *Science*, 1974, **183**, 482–488.

Smith, Frank. *Understanding Reading.* New York: Holt, Rinehart & Winston, 1971; Second edition, 1978; Third edition, 1982. (a)

Smith, Frank. *Psycholinguistics and Reading.* New York: Holt, Rinehart & Winston, 1973.

Smith, Frank. *Comprehension and Learning.* New York: Holt, Rinehart & Winston, 1975. (a)

Smith, Frank. The role of prediction in reading. *Elementary English*, 1975, **52**, 305–311. (b)

Smith, Frank. Making sense of language learning. In Fanselow, John F. and Clymes, Ruth H. (Eds.), *On TESOL '76.* Washington, DC: Teachers of English to Speakers of Other Languages, 1976.

Smith, Frank. *Writing and the Writer.* New York: Holt, Rinehart & Winston, 1982. (b)

Smith, Frank and Goodman, Kenneth S. On the psycholinguistic method of teaching reading. *Elementary School Journal*, 1971, **71**, 177–181.

Smith, Frank and Holmes, Deborah Lott. The independence of letter, word and meaning identification in reading. *Reading Research Quarterly*, 1971, **6**, 394–415.

Stebbins, L. B.; St. Pierre, R. G.; Proper, E. C.; Anderson, R. B.; and Cerva, T. R. *Education as Experimentation: A Planned Variation Model: Vol. LV-A An Evaluation of Follow-Through.* Cambridge, MA: Abt Associates, 1977.

Sutton-Smith, Brian (Ed.) *Play and Learning.* New York: Gardner, 1979.

Thorndike, E. L. and Lorge, I. *The Teacher's Word Book of 30,000 Words.* New York: Teachers College, 1944.

Torrey, Jane W. Illiteracy in the ghetto. *Harvard Educational Review*, 1970, **40**, 2, 253–259.

Torrey, Jane W. Reading that comes naturally: The early reader. In Walker, T. G. and MacKinnon, G. E. (Eds.), *Reading Research: Advances in Theory and Practice* (Vol. 1). New York: Academic Press, 1979.

Tough, Joan. *Talking and Learning.* London, Ward Lock: 1977.

Tulving, Endel and Gold, Cecille. Stimulus information and contextual information as determinants of tachistoscopic recognition of words. *Journal of Experimental Psychology*, 1963, **66**, 4, 319–327.

Tulving, Endel and Thomson, Donald M. Encoding specificity and retrieval processes in episodic memory. *Psychological Review*, 1973, **80**, 352–373.

Venezky, Richard L. English orthography: Its graphical structure and its relation to sound. *Reading Research Quarterly*, 1967, **2**, 75–106.

Venezky, Richard L. *The Structure of English Orthography.* The Hague: Mouton, 1970.

Vygotsky, Lev S. *Thought and Language.* Cambridge, MA: MIT Press, 1962.

Weir, Ruth H. *Language in the Crib.* The Hague, Mouton: 1962.

Williams, Joanna. Reading instruction today. *American Psychologist*, 1979, **34**, 917–922.

Ylisto, Ingrid P. Early reading responses of young Finnish children. *The Reading Teacher*, 1977, **31**, 167–172.

Name Index

Subject Index